ISRAEL'S POETRY OF RESISTANCE

ISRAEL'S POETRY OF RESISTANCE

AFRICANA PERSPECTIVES ON EARLY HEBREW VERSE

HUGH R. PAGE JR.

Fortress Press
Minneapolis

ISRAEL'S POETRY OF RESISTANCE

Africana Perspectives on Early Hebrew Verse

Cover image: *The Baptism*, Romare Bearden © Romare Bearden Foundation/Licensed by VAGA, New York, NY

Cover design: Laurie Ingram

Library of Congress Cataloging-in-Publication Data is available

Print ISBN: 978-0-8006-6334-6

eBook ISBN: 978-1-4514-2628-1

The paper used in this publication meets the minimum requirements of American National Standard for Information Sciences — Permanence of Paper for Printed Library Materials, ANSI Z329.48-1984.

Manufactured in the U.S.A.

This book was produced using PressBooks.com, and PDF rendering was done by PrinceXML.

For my parents
Deacons Hugh R. Page Sr.
and Dr. Elaine B. Page
who planted and nurtured
the dreams realized in these pages
and my partner
Dr. Jacquetta E. Page
whose embrace assures me that
love is indeed "as strong as death itself"
Song of Songs 8:6

CONTENTS

Part III. Preaching, Teaching, and Living Early Hebrew Poems

PREFACE

When I first conceived of the project leading to this book, back in 1996, I hoped simply to extend the research begun in the 1950s by Frank Moore Cross Jr. and David Noel Freedman[1] and continued in the subsequent postscript to their dissertation, written some four decades later.[2] However, strange things happened along the way, not the least of which was the realization that all encounters with Scripture are contingent and that acknowledgment of authorial location is essential, rather than detrimental, to biblical scholarship. This moment of clarity radically reshaped the contours of the original proposal and led to the current volume: a conversation between ancient Hebrew poems and selected Africana cultural artifacts. It is very much in the vein of the context-specific reading strategies advocated most recently in *The Africana Bible* (2010) and in my own essay on early Hebrew poetry included in it.[3]

The earliest subgroup of biblical poems (Exodus 15; Psalm 29; Judges 5; Genesis 49; Numbers 23–24; Deuteronomy 32 and 33; 1 Samuel 2; 2 Samuel 1, 22 (= Psalm 18), and 23; and Psalms 68, 72, and 78) has much to say to the Africana community living in the North American Diaspora. Approaching them as a subcanon, with its own distinctive ideological parameters and theological foci, Black pastors, preachers, and Bible readers will discover in these poems prisms that refract the history and cultural norms of early Israel for a twenty-first-century audience. As a distinct collection within the Hebrew Bible / Old Testament / First Testament, early Hebrew poetry preserves the inspired insights of Israel's most ancient griots. It represents the earliest recorded musings of our biblical forebears on God, the universe, community, nature, humanity, and life's ultimate meaning.[4] Moreover, it offers a selective view of an Israelite ethos, born in crisis, that is dynamic, creative, pluriform, polyphonic, and transgressive. This is a community whose early challenges were not unlike those encountered by many Africana peoples today, particularly those dealing with the effects of social displacement and marginalization.

These poems are best seen as a literary assemblage that mirrors the trauma of the community whose artists produced it. Their collection, curating, and preservation within early Israel was, I believe, an act of prayerful resistance: a communal *no* to the forces of despair and a collective *yes* to the power of the Spirit. Consequently, they deal with the realities of a culturally diverse community experiencing transition and loss while struggling to define itself. No aspect of daily existence, no human emotion, is left unexplored. Some of the poems are raw. A few are esoteric. All are real.

The poems are at once speculative and concrete in dealing with issues cosmic and pragmatic. That reflection on the formative years of the tribal confederacy and the early monarchy is cast in verse is indicative of the premium placed on the power of expressive culture in ancient Israel—music, dance, and artful speech in particular. Moreover, that these works of verbal artistry have been strategically placed in each of the Hebrew Bible's canonical subdivisions—Torah, Prophets, and Writings—is significant. It suggests that Israel's most ancient poetic reminiscences were held to be not only cultural treasures but also eschatologizing texts capable of bringing people into communion with one another and their deity. Moreover, it implies that Israel's early poets were esteemed, by their contemporaries and later generations, as literary, social, and numinous *makers*.

The adaptive lifeways and ideas reflected in their works resonate with those in the Africana community who find themselves perennially outside of the social or political mainstream. Therefore, as theological, pastoral, and political interlocutors, early Hebrew poems have much to commend with regard to the creation of Africana spiritualities of resistance today. Reading them from a perspective that is decidedly African American allows them to speak in an idiom understandable at once to those at home within the North American Diaspora and to others for whom separation from a homeland—whether actual, imagined, or longed for—is a distinctive marker of identity.

Unfortunately, scholarly consensus about the origins of Israel has yet to emerge. What John McDermott concluded in his brief popular survey some time ago holds true today, namely, that "the evidence we have is open to various interpretations" and that the mystery of Israel's origin remains unsolved.[5] The reliability of the Bible as primary witness to this formative process is no longer presumed to be unassailable.[6] Although the current study cannot bring closure to this knotty debate, it is hoped that it will demonstrate how self-conscious contextual reading of what are purportedly some of its most ancient primary literary sources may help us to think about this conundrum in new ways. Thus, it is my hope that this volume will do for the study of early Israel and its poetry of resistance what Julio Finn's *The Bluesman: The Musical Heritage of Black Men and Women in the Americas* (1992) did for the study of another genre born of struggle, blues songs, that is, to promote a vision of them as not simply texts "but a way of life."[7] Taking Finn's lead, my goal is also subtly to mirror the "rhythm," "pitch," and "images and dynamics"[8] of both early Hebrew poems and Africana life in engaging them.

What follows, therefore, is not an exhaustive rehash of earlier scholarship on this subject. It is, instead, a compendium of autobiographical reflections on Scripture in the vein of those found in Jeffrey Staley's pioneering work; what Norman Denzin might classify as a "Reflexive, Messy Text"; an exercise in both biblical scholarship and constructive theology built on the paradigm of conjure proposed more than a decade ago by Theophus Smith—one that, to borrow his words, "allows its engagement with biblical hermeneutics to be displayed to clear view"; an early twenty-first-century response to Ishmael Reed's "Neo-HooDoo Manifesto"; an excavation of ancient Hebrew verse that, in the spirit of bell hooks's *Bone Black*, is presented as "truth and myth—as poetic witness"; a new kind of critical edition of these poems that implicitly says yes to Vincent Wimbush's call to be a runaway member of the guild of biblicists—a state, in his words, of "marronage, running away with an attitude and a plan, a taking flight—in body, but even more importantly in terms of consciousness."[9]

I thank the late David Noel Freedman and Frank Moore Cross Jr.—mentors both—for their encouragement and helpful suggestions throughout the many years during which the very earliest stage of the work leading to the production of this monograph was unfolding. I also thank my father, the late Deacon Hugh R. Page Sr., and my mother, Deacon Elaine B. Page, for believing and investing in my dreams; and my wife, Dr. Jacquetta E. Page, who is—and will forever be—my muse, fellow traveler, and soul mate.

Hugh Rowland Page Jr.

Notes

1. Frank Moore Cross and David Noel Freedman, *Early Hebrew Orthography*, ed. J. B. Pritchard. American Oriental Series 36 (New Haven, CT: American Oriental Society, 1952).

2. Frank Moore Cross and David Noel Freedman, *Studies in Ancient Yahwistic Poetry*, 2nd ed., Biblical Resource Series (Grand Rapids, MI: Eerdmans, 1997).

3. Hugh R. Page Jr. et al., eds., *The Africana Bible: Reading Israel's Scriptures from Africa and the African Diaspora* (Minneapolis: Fortress Press, 2010); Hugh R. Page Jr., "Early Hebrew Poetry and Ancient Pre-Biblical Sources," in Page et al., *Africana Bible.*

4. For a variety of reasons—linguistic, thematic, prosodic, and other—I am of the opinion that the poems are in fact archaic (legitimately old) rather than archaizing (displaying literary features that lead one to believe that they are old). I concur with Freedman's assessment almost two

decades ago that such a conclusion could be based not on "proof beyond a reasonable doubt" but on "the preponderance of the evidence and a rational reconstruction of the contents of the poems and their meaning." Cross and Freedman, *Studies in Ancient Yahwistic Poetry*, x.

5. John J. McDermott, *What Are They Saying about the Formation of Israel?* What Are They Saying About Series (Mahwah, NJ: Paulist, 1998), 92.

6. Among those arguing for the primacy of material remains other than the Hebrew Bible in the writing of a history of Israel, William Dever's recent reconstruction of eighth-century BCE life reminds readers that the texts of this period not only are "relatively late, elitist, and tendentious," but have little to do with the day-to-day lives of either common folk or women as well. William Dever, *The Lives of Ordinary People in Ancient Israel: Where Archaeology and the Bible Intersect* (Grand Rapids, MI: Eerdmans, 2012), 10, and ch. 1, n. 20.

7. Julio Finn, *The Bluesman: The Musical Heritage of Black Men and Women in the Americas* (New York: Interlink, 1992), 2.

8. Ibid.

9. Jeffrey L. Staley, *Reading with a Passion: Rhetoric, Autobiography, and the American West in the Gospel of John* (New York: Continuum, 1995); Norman Denzin, *Interpretive Ethnography: Ethnographic Practices for the 21st Century* (Thousand Oaks, CA: Sage, 1997), 224; Theophus Smith, *Conjuring Culture: Biblical Formations of Black America* (New York: Oxford University Press, 1994), 10; Ishmael Reed, *Conjure* (Amherst: University of Massachusetts Press, 1972), 20–25; bell hooks, *Bone Black: Memories of Girlhood* (New York: Holt, 1996), xiv; Vincent Wimbush, "Interpreters: Enslaving/Enslaved/Runagate," *Journal of Biblical Literature* 130, no. 1 (2011): 17.

PART I

The Bible and Africana Reality

Wilson Park, Homewood, and Early Hebrew Verse

An Africana Perspective on the Albright Tradition

*The predicament of the Black intellectual
need not be grim and dismal. Despite the
pervasive racism of American society and
anti-intellectualism of the Black
Community, critical space and insurgent
activity can be expanded. This expansion
will occur more readily when Black
intellectuals take a more candid look at
themselves, the historical and social forces
that shape them, and the limited though
significant resources from whence they
come.*

——Cornel West, *Breaking Bread:
Insurgent Black Intellectual Life*
(with bell hooks)

Interest in the examination of Israel's earliest verse and its cultural setting
can be said to have reached a particular zenith in the last half of the twentieth
century with the work of scholars inheriting the intellectual mantle from the
late William F. Albright and two of his major pupils, the late Frank Moore
Cross Jr. and the late David Noel Freedman. Within this tradition, issues such as
sequence dating; orthography; prosodic conventions; divine names, titles, and
epithets; periodization; historical reconstruction; and theology were of primary

importance. Among those continuing to labor in this metaphorical vineyard, the current author included, their efforts remain foundational. However, outside of this circle of researchers, opinion has been divided as to the legitimacy and enduring value of the study of early Hebrew verse. Among the more significant shortcomings cited are the impact of Albright's religious beliefs on his interpretation and dating of the poems and the question of whether extant linguistic data can be used to distinguish between truly archaic and archaizing texts in the Hebrew Bible.[1]

My own fascination with early Hebrew poetry and subsequent grafting onto the Albright lineage are odd and paradoxical, especially given that the "Oriental Seminary" where the groundwork for this research was laid is on the campus of Johns Hopkins University, a five-minute drive from the less-than-tony neighborhood of Baltimore in which I spent my youth. Our home, 507 East Cold Spring Lane, was just on "the other side" of York Road, what some considered the dividing line between the fringe of ritzy Guilford—at one time racially restricted—and our working-class enclave of Wilson Park. Both Wilson Park and Guilford were a stone's throw away from Johns Hopkins's Homewood campus.[2] While Albright and his students labored over sequence dating, paleography, orthography, and prosody, many of the people I knew pondered why it was that Hopkins remained such a foreboding place, even for the gifted children of the "talented tenth."[3]

Several of Albright's students would later become either my teachers (such as Cross and William Moran) or my senior mentors at a distance (Freedman). They trained there before I was conceived and when I was a child. Their Baltimore and mine were not remotely the same. Their Hopkins was, for me, terra incognita. Its world-renowned medical school and hospital were themselves held by many to be exploitative forces in the city's poorer neighborhoods.[4] Even as a high school senior, I neither dreamed of attending nor thought of applying to be a student there. Like many of the state and private colleges and universities in Maryland, it was not perceived to be a welcoming place for African American students and had precious few Black faculty members.[5]

That I should have any interest whatsoever in, let alone an abiding passion for, a stream of research whose headwaters can be traced to such an environment is for me a source of endless wonderment. It developed, of course, long after Albright's passing and during my own years of graduate study at Harvard (1984–1990). It troubles me to look critically at my relationship to it. To raise discomfiting questions about it is likely to strike some as disloyal. However, given what Cornel West has said, in the epigraph to this chapter, about the values informing the work of the insurgent Black intellectual, a mantle I don with some degree of trepidation, it seems vital. It is perhaps better to think of mine as an "indecent" theological intervention aimed at discovering a deeper connection between early Israel and Wilson Park: a linkage that helped shape my academic vocation and make me a mediator between the Albright tradition and my neighbors on Cold Spring Lane and the other largely segregated streets on which I walked as child and young adult.[6] It is an agenda that resonates with the at-times-countercultural and antiauthoritarian spirit that imbues early Hebrew poetry itself.

Acknowledging this life experience and using it as a starting point from which to engage these poems also allows me to work within the philological parameters proposed by Hans Ulrich Gumbrecht and delimit, edit, offer commentary on, provide a historical context for, and curate this corpus of poems in a manner that both calls attention to its implicit difficulties and facilitates a reading of it that is multifaceted and rich.[7] The placing of certain contextually specific Africana concerns front and center, in so doing, promises to yield intentionally "messy editions" of these poems—that is, curated versions that juxtapose them with contemporary poetry, memoir, fiction, and African American music—that stimulate more intense and evocative thinking about their implications for marginalized people of color worldwide.[8] Gumbrecht's advice here is poignant in this regard. He advocates the production of textual editions that open the door to encounters that move beyond simple translational code breaking and toward what he describes as "both joyful and painful oscillation between losing and regaining intellectual control or orientation."[9] For him, the success of such a paradigm for reading is dependent on a philologist's ability to curate texts that elicit discomfort. Of such work and such reading, he says: "For the higher the philological quality of an edition, we can say, the more disorienting, challenging, and complex the reading (and the *Reading*) that it informs will turn out to be."[10] The value of a well-edited text is found, therefore, not in the false comfort derived from an erroneous belief that it has been expertly mastered but in its capacity to generate in the reader an abiding appreciation of its implicit dynamism, the imaginative capacities of the editor, and the artifact's "untamed complexity."[11] Bringing early Hebrew poetry into conversation with Africana life certainly promises to foster such productive disorientation and strengthen the body of research on the former to date.[12]

The study of Hebrew poetry is fraught with linguistic and methodological problems. Early on, the distinguishing markers of poetry, prose, and verse; prosodic conventions; and parallelism were of great interest to students of

Hebrew verse. In recent years, issues even more vexing than the aforementioned have been enumerated, among which are the impact of poetic theory—ancient and modern—on existing definitions of poetry; the selection of literary texts with which to compare the Hebrew Bible's poetic corpus; the theories informing the work of major scholars who have contributed to our understanding of Hebrew poetry; the impact of approaches such as ethnopoetics, sociopoetics, and reflexive ethnography on both the identification and the interpretation of biblical poetry; and the impulses (including social, psychological, and physiological) that are generative of verse and their bearing on our understanding of the genre and its progenitors.

Among the questions raised by prior scholarship within the Albright tradition relating specifically to early Hebrew poetry are the following:

1. Is the poetry, in fact, early? How do we know it is early? What characteristics can be identified to establish its antiquity (content, prosody, orthography, theology, and so on)?

2. What is this poetry's value to the larger enterprise of critical biblical study? Does it help in the source-critical debate? In what ways does it contribute to the agenda of Hermann Gunkel and other form critics? How does the corpus inform our understanding of early Israelite theology?

3. How are the poems to be read— literally, symbolically, impressionistically, or otherwise?

4. How do we assess the quantity and quality of cultural and historical data found in the poems?

5. Are the poems merely scattered compositions from a variety of sources, or did they at any time belong to a single collection?

6. What can be said of the poems' canonical function in light of their current placement (Torah, 6; Prophets, 4; and Writings, 5)?

7. To what extent is comparison of these fifteen poems with other poetic compositions (such as Homeric verse, Sumero-Akkadian myth, Egyptian folklore, and Indo-European epic) useful?

8. What, if anything, does early Hebrew poetry have the ability to tell us about: Israelite origins, basic features of ancient Israelite religion, social life in ancient Syro-Palestine during the thirteenth through tenth centuries BCE?

9. How are these poems related to other embedded narrative poems found in the Hebrew Bible?

10. What can be said of ancient Hebrew prosody? How important is it to our understanding of early Hebrew poetry?

11. From an orthographic perspective, do the poems reflect practices earlier than the remaining literature within the Masoretic Text of the Hebrew Bible? Were the poems written in a distinct dialect of Hebrew?

12. Have the poems been preserved by later editors in more or less pristine condition?

Although progress has been made in addressing many of the aforementioned questions, there is considerable work yet to be done.

In previous essays, I have explored several of these topics, as well as others, directly or indirectly related to early Hebrew poems. These include their possible use as an artfully constructed repository of cultural realia; the problematic nature of traditional paradigms for understanding Israel's origins; how the most ancient stratum of these poems might be read in light of a theological focus on the poor and disenfranchised; the deployment of post-Katrina blues poems as interlocutors with these poems; the light shed on them by African American bric-a-brac; and the role of conscious collection and curatorial efforts in their assemblage in the Hebrew Bible.[13] These exploratory forays have allowed me to test interpretive models both traditional and experimental. Through them, I have come to a deeper appreciation of the poems' idiosyncrasies and the windows they open onto the ancient world in which they were composed.

The current volume seeks to build on this existing body of work by offering critical and creative interventions that bring early Hebrew poetry into contact with selected literary, artistic, and other artifacts from the Africana world, thereby shedding additional light on the poems and the approaches used to read them in such a milieu. It is also hoped that this approach will advance the aims of that body of work assembled in *The Africana Bible* (2010) and will define in greater detail the parameters of that developing subfield known as Africana biblical studies.[14] I will incorporate a convention already at home in some traditions of ethnographic writing that blurs the boundary between traditional modes of scholarly writing and art, while at the same time making clear the social location from which my own research comes. A close reading of the work of many pioneering figures in biblical and cognate research reveals that such reflexive elements have never been absent from writing in biblical studies and cognate fields.[15] One often finds hints about authorial identity and setting, and the impact that these have on methodology and conclusions, in prefatory notes, parenthetical remarks, footnotes, endnotes, and, on occasion, biographies.

It would not be inaccurate to say that my first formal interest in Hebrew poetry as a topic of inquiry began in a smoke-filled office at General

Theological Seminary.[16] It was in this sanctuary that I, along with several other MDiv and STM students, learned three things: the "art" of rhetorical criticism and its impact on hermeneutics and historical-critical work; the relationship of rhetorical criticism to Hermann Gunkel's larger interest in both the history and the social location of ancient Israel's literary *Gattungen*; and the interplay between established form and individual "markers of genius" in the production of ancient and modern texts. It was there that I also gained an appreciation of the subtle conventions and rich textures of Hebrew verse, as well as the importance of charting significant features of poetic artifice and exploring their semantic implications.[17]

Equally true is the fact that the stage was set for this exploration of ancient biblical poetry many years earlier while I was learning to negotiate the strange racial boundaries that circumscribed the lives of Black youth in Baltimore from the mid-1950s to the early 1970s. Ours was, and is, a city of neighborhoods. Many of them have been and remain racially or ethnically distinct. Some witnessed major demographic transitions during the 1960s. Wilson Park was one such neighborhood. Ours was one of the first Black families to move onto the 500 block of East Cold Spring Lane. Within a decade, no White families remained. Flight to the outlying suburbs was in full swing. Ours gradually became a safe and stable block of Black middle-class homeowners who shared many of the same values and looked out for one another's homes and children. Tragically, the same was not true in all quarters of Wilson Park. As in many other areas of the city, drugs, theft, and random violence became increasingly prevalent. Today, the neighborhood, like many other largely African American neighborhoods in the city, is deteriorating. The same is true, by and large, of the other Black neighborhood where I spent most of my youth: West Baltimore's Sandtown-Winchester.

We spent a good deal of time in that part of the city. My parents grew up there: one on Mount Street, the other on Westwood Avenue. I knew its main and side streets more intimately than those at home. We called our regular trek from Cold Spring Lane to my grandparents' homes or to church "going into town." Interestingly enough, that trip almost always took us through Guilford and directly by the Johns Hopkins campus. We'd drive down Charles Street by the Episcopal Cathedral of the Incarnation and the university's east gate. Nestled in the middle of campus, obscured from our view by the Eisenhower Library, was Gilman Hall, home of the "Oriental Seminary" and Albright's Baltimore school of ancient Near Eastern studies. I had no inkling that anyone or anything affiliated with Hopkins would have an impact on my future. At times, I would wonder why it seemed that only a handful or so of local African Americans had any formal affiliation with the school, as students, staff, faculty, or physicians who had privileges at the Johns Hopkins Hospital. I'd often look at the faces traversing the campus and wonder, as we passed by on those drives, if I'd see any that looked like me. That was a rare occurrence in those days.

Little did I know that my relationship with both Guilford and Hopkins would change and become much more complex. In June 1980, I would lay prostrate on the floor of the cathedral, in which Albright's funeral was conducted, before taking my vows for diaconal ordination. Raised in a strongly Baptist family, I'd followed the lead of one of my uncles and converted to Anglicanism. By that time, I'd also decided that I wanted to be a Hebrew Bible scholar. That decision was met with some surprise by several of my African American seminary peers, who at that point knew of very few Blacks in the field.[18]

In 1984, while working as an interim priest in a Detroit parish, I would drive to Ann Arbor and have a delightful conversation with David Noel Freedman about my interest in the study of the ancient Near East. I was completely taken aback by his kindness and openness to my possibly coming to the University of Michigan to work on a PhD with him. I've never forgotten that. Later that year, I would accept an offer to enter Harvard's doctoral program in Near Eastern Languages and Civilizations (NELC), a decision that would graft me onto the intellectual lineage of Albright and his own teacher, Paul Haupt. Through lectures and unofficial back channels, I became privy to the "lore of the tribe." I heard about the tiffs within its several "clans." I came to know which scholars in the larger field of biblical studies were "insiders" whose opinions could be trusted. I also familiarized myself very quickly with the names of those whose research was considered unimportant, outside the mainstream, suspect, or highly tendentious. I followed closely the return to prominence of the program in ancient Near Eastern studies at Hopkins in the late 1980s and selected, for the focus of my dissertation at Harvard, a topic given to Frank Cross by Albright on one of his doctoral examinations. An expanded version of that project would evolve into my first book. Perhaps most importantly, I rediscovered my love of poetry and developed a passion for the study of early Hebrew poems.

This rekindling of my courtship with poetry came, oddly enough, through three flashes of insight. The first occurred when I read Cross's article on the prosodic structure of the first chapter of the book of Lamentations and realized how heavily his own understanding of the way parallelism worked was influenced by the thought of the linguist and poet Roman Jakobson.[19] I had a series of secondary "aha" moments in a seminar with James Kugel, whose understanding of Hebrew prosody was informed by his linguistic training and his life experience as a literary editor and practicing poet (Kugel was poetry editor for *Harper's Magazine* from 1972 to 1974). It was at this time that I began to realize that an important strategy for engaging ancient poetry, both biblical and nonbiblical, was to do so as philologist *and* poet. This would involve intentionally making the boundaries between grammatical analysis, scansion, hermeneutics, and poem making more porous. The third and final moment of inspiration came as I discovered kindred intellectual spirits, past and present, who shed light on ancient Hebrew life and literature through the use of comparative mythology and folklore, ethnology, Serbo-Croatian poetry, and Homeric epic. For several of these scholars, early biblical poems held the key to understanding Israel's origins and musings about the divine.

I was also influenced by another set of voices, whose presence I would not be able fully to acknowledge until recently: African American visual artists, poets, and songwriters. They were the *loas* (or spirits) hovering in the background of so much of my work. Prince's "The Ladder," "Hold Me," by Whitney Houston and Teddy Pendergrass, and Michael Jackson's "Man in the Mirror" were my silent partners in conversations with *Gilgamesh*, *Atrahasis*, and the story of "Dawn and Dusk" in Ugaritic lore. Morris Day's song "Daydreaming," and Terence Trent D'Arby's "If You All Get to Heaven" were part of the soundtrack for my comprehensive-exam preparation in Hebrew and Akkadian. I recall not being able to get Billy Paul's song "War of the Gods" out of my head as I made final revisions on my first academic book, *The Myth of Cosmic Rebellion* (1996), and prepared to send it to press.[20] Even now, as I ponder the role of figures such as Moses and Balaam in Israel's most ancient verse, scenes from Zora Neale Hurston's *Mules and Men* flash before me,[21] and I hear the refrain, "I'm a man," from Muddy Waters's "Mannish Boy." When I read Judges 5 and think of Deborah and Jael, I hear Koko Taylor's strong voice singing in "Voodoo Woman":

> They call me the voodoo woman
> And I know the reason why
> Lord, if I raise my name
> You know, the sky begin to cry.[22]

The decade of conversations and editorial planning culminating in the publication of *The Africana Bible* assuaged any guilty feelings I might have had about owning these influences. I realized that scholars would do well to acknowledge openly the muses and orishas who inspire them, rather than concealing them in footnotes, referencing them in memoirs, or disclosing them in cocktail banter at the meetings of professional societies. As for scholars hailing from Africa and the African Diaspora, we must be free unashamedly to name those sources of inspiration that come from our own milieu. This is one of the distinguishing markers of Africana biblical criticism.

So, at this juncture, I can honestly say that Wilson Park, Sandtown-Winchester, and the drive "in town" raise a multiplicity of questions about the Albright–Hopkins tradition of scholarship on early Hebrew poetry, particularly its theological underpinnings, grounded as they are in Albright's fundamental confidence in the historical and cultural trustworthiness of these ancient poems, especially the extent to which they can be said to convey essential truths while maintaining a high degree of historical reliability.[23] Such an assertion helps shore up the footing of odd interdisciplinary endeavors such as biblical studies and biblical archeology, particularly within the confines of the modern research university. However, given that the earliest stratum of these poems was likely produced in the social maelstrom that witnessed the collapse of Syro-Palestinian urban enclaves during the late Bronze and early Iron Ages, one wonders whether the artistic canons in the newly developing and recently displaced social groups where early Hebrew verse flowered would have placed a premium on indirect speech, concealment, double entendre, and word games as survival techniques.

Such modes of communication were standard fare on Willow Avenue, Bruce Street, and the other thoroughfares crisscrossing the enclaves of the comparably dislocated and dispossessed in Baltimore. In such an environment, one noted but read between the lines of texts, both oral and written. History and truth were important, but so was attentiveness to the contingent nature of all supposedly authoritative—and often racialized—narratives. The backstory or subtext of anything and everything might not be found in the distant past or even in a contemporary cultural inversion; the particulars could be hidden in plain sight, set a bit "off center" so that one had to pay close attention to the *margins* in order to see them.

Had there been a closer connection between the world of the "Oriental Seminary" at Johns Hopkins and that of Wilson Park and Sandtown-Winchester, I suspect Albright and at least some of his early students might have accessed oral histories of Black women and men who migrated from North Carolina and Virginia to Maryland in their reading of Exodus 15; or the story of Harriet Tubman to offer a layered assessment of the encounter between Sisera and Jael. In the late 1970s, inheritors of the tradition might have frequented, conducted fieldwork at, and published their findings on oral lore gathered from one or more of Baltimore's candle shops—Old Grandpa, or Grandma's Candle Shop, an easy walk from Lexington Market—to parse the ambiguous figure of Balaam in light of the materia medica and praxis of African American divination and healing.[24] In so doing, they might have come to realize, as I have, that such places cast light on how communities under duress preserve, conceal, and selectively reveal their most revered traditions in numbers, potions, songs, and ḥîdôt minnî-qedem ("ancient riddles"; Ps. 78:2). Perhaps it is this lacuna that fate has left me to fill. To do so means building a spiritual bridge between Guilford, Harvard, and the communitas Africana, a bridge that I hope will establish a new and lasting détente between these worlds.

Notes

1. See, for example, Burke O. Long, *Planting and Reaping Albright: Politics, Ideology, and Interpreting the Bible* (University Park: Pennsylvania State University Press, 1997).

2. On Baltimore's tortured history of segregated neighborhoods and housing, see Antero Pietila, *Not in My Neighborhood: How Bigotry Shaped a Great American City* (Chicago: Dee, 2010).

3. On this concept, see Lawrence R. Rodgers, "The Talented Tenth," in *Africana: The Encyclopedia of the African and African American Experience*, ed. H. L. Kwame Anthony Appiah and Henry Louis Gates Jr., 2nd ed. (New York: Oxford University Press, 2005).

4. This was at a time long before knowledge of the tragic case of Henrietta Lacks; see Rebecca Skloot, *The Immortal Life of Henrietta Lacks* (New York: Crown, 2010).

5. For a history of African Americans at Johns Hopkins University, see the online gallery "African Americans @ Johns Hopkins University," maintained at http://afam.nts.jhu.edu/about.

6. On "indecent theology," see Marcella Althaus-Reid, *Indecent Theology: Theological Perversions in Sex, Gender, and Politics* (London: Routledge, 2000).

7. Hans Ulrich Gumbrecht, *The Powers of Philology: Dynamics of Textual Scholarship* (Urbana: University of Illinois Press, 2003), 3.

8. On "messy texts," see Denzin, *Interpretive Ethnography*, xvii–xviii, 224–27. A recent work that could well be categorized as a "messy edition" because of the very creative and unusual approach taken to translation and presentation—i.e., through the medium of jazz—is that of the "Song to Inanna" prepared by Cass Dalglish, in *Humming the Blues* (Corvalis, OR: Calyx, 2008).

9. Gumbrecht, *Powers of Philology*, 85.

10. Ibid.

11. Ibid., 7.

12. This can be enhanced by a translation of the poetry that is, at its core, equally provocative. Such will be the approach I take. Here, I follow the lead of the late Simon Parker, who was fully in favor of such experimentation. Simon Parker, "Toward Literary Translations of Ugaritic Poetry," *Ugarit-Forschungen* 22 (1990): 257–70.

13. See, respectively, Hugh R. Page Jr., "Ethnological Criticism: An Apologia and Application," in *Exploring New Paradigms in Biblical and Cognate Studies*, ed. Hugh R. Page Jr. (Lewiston, NY: Mellen Biblical Press, 1996); "Myth, Meta-Narrative, and Historical Reconstruction: Rethinking the Nature of Scholarship on Israelite Origins," in *Studies in the Hebrew Bible, Qumran, and the Septuagint Presented to Eugene Ulrich*, ed. Peter W. Flint, Emanuel Tov, and James C. VanderKam (Leiden, Neth.: Brill, 2006); "Toward the Creation of Transformational Spiritualities: Re-Engaging Israel's Early Poetic Tradition in Light of the

Church's Preferential Option for the Poor," in *The Option for the Poor in Christian Theology*, ed. Daniel G. Groody (Notre Dame, IN: University of Notre Dame Press, 2007); *A Teacher for all Generations: Essays in Honor of James C. Vanderkam*, ed. Eric F. Mason, Samuel I. Thomas, Alison Schofield, and Eugene Ulrich, vol. 1. Supplements to the Journal for the Study of Judaism, volume 153/1 (Leiden: E. J. Brill, 2012): 37–47; "Early Hebrew Poetry and Ancient Pre-Biblical Sources," in *The Africana Bible: Reading Israel's Scriptures from Africa and the African Diaspora*, ed. Hugh R. Page Jr. et al. (Minneapolis: Fortress Press, 2010); and "Myth and Social Realia in Ancient Israel: Early Hebrew Poems as Folkloric Assemblage," in *Myth and Scripture: Contemporary Perspectives on Religion, Language, and Imagination*, ed. J. Dexter E. Callender (Atlanta, GA: Society of Biblical Literature, forthcoming).

14. Page et al., *Africana Bible*.

15. For example, a great deal can be gleaned about the role that Albright's personal religious faith, proficiency as linguistic autodidact, and doctoral student under the tutelage of Paul Haupt had on his approach to philology and pedagogy from the very illuminating biography written by Leona Glidden Running and David Noel Freedman, *William Foxwell Albright: A 20th Century Genius* (1975; repr., Berrien Springs, MI: Andrews University Press, 1991). The impact that these experiences had on Cross and Freedman can likewise be seen in a variety of published documents (scholarly publications, homilies, etc.), personal correspondence, and oral lore that offer a glimpse into their professional praxis and approaches to teaching. The autobiographies of Samuel Noah Kramer, *In the World of Sumer: An Autobiography* (Detroit, MI: Wayne State University Press, 1988), and Cyrus Herzl Gordon, *A Scholar's Odyssey*, Biblical Scholarship in North America 20 (Atlanta, GA: Society of Biblical Literature, 2000), offer comparably interesting perspectives on the life and work of these luminaries in ancient Near Eastern studies.

16. This was during the 1982–83 academic year under the tutelage of Richard W. Corney, a student of the late James Muilenburg.

17. I describe this process, other scholarly influences, and their relationship to the praxis of scholarship and ministry in Hugh R. Page Jr., "Performance as Interpretive Metaphor: The Bible as Libretto for Research, Translation, Preaching, and Spirituality in the 21st Century; Prolegomenon," *Memphis Theological Seminary Journal* 41 (2005):13–20.

18. In the 1970s, there had been one African American who was an Episcopalian: Robert A. Bennett. Fortunately, he happened to be a Baltimorean, a priest, and a scholar trained in the Albright tradition at Harvard. He would in due course become a trusted friend and early mentor of mine.

19. Frank Moore Cross, "Studies in the Structure of Hebrew Verse: The Prosody of Lamentations 1:1-22," in *The Word of the Lord Shall Go Forth: Essays in Honor of David Noel Freedman*, ed. Carol L. Meyers and M. O'Connor (Winona Lake, IN: Eisenbrauns, 1983).

20. Hugh R. Page Jr., *The Myth of Cosmic Rebellion: A Study of Its Reflexes in Ugaritic and Biblical Literature*. Supplements to *Vetus Testamentum* 65 (Leiden, Neth.: Brill, 1996).

21. Zora Neale Hurston, *Mules and Men* (1935; repr., New York: HarperPerennial, 1990).

22. Koko Taylor, "Voodoo Woman," *I Got What it Takes*. Alligator Records, compact disc. Originally released 1975.

23. See, in particular, the comments in William F. Albright, "Archeology Confronts Biblical Criticism," *American Scholar* 7, no. 2 (1938): 176–88.

24. Strangely enough, Albright himself seems to have valued and embraced at least one folk-healing practice: that of the mustard plaster (see Running and Freedman, *William Foxwell Albright*, 212–13). One wonders whether he also understood some of the traditions regarding the spiritual properties associated with mustard seeds in African American lore; see, for example, Catherine Yronwode, *Hoodoo Herb and Root Magic: A Materia Magica of African-American Conjure* (Forestville, CA: Lucky Mojo Curio Co., 2002), 137.

2

Diasporas and Adaptive Strategies in Early Hebrew Verse and the Africana World

The preservation of early Hebrew poetry was, in part, a project undertaken in the Jewish Diaspora of the sixth and fifth centuries BCE. The poems involved were part of the several collections that eventually became the anthology we now know as the Tanak. The extent to which exilic editors deemed any one or more of these poems particularly ancient is not known. The collection and editing of the corpus likely began much earlier, though the various stages in the process are impossible to chart. One assertion that can be made with confidence is that the curating of the poems, and of the Hebrew Bible as a whole, was a means of dealing with at least some of the uncertainties associated with living in dispersion and under foreign domination. Whether they are physical, emotional, spiritual, imagined, eschatological, or of some other type, diasporas require complex negotiations between locations and social groups. Removal from an actual or illusory homeland, through either coercion or voluntary relocation, is often an occasion for rethinking identity. It can also lead to a reassessment of the relationship between those living remotely and the kin they have left behind. Feelings of grief, loss, and disorientation are not uncommon by-products of such an experience.

Diasporas can also be dangerous. Living as a first-, second-, or third-generation "stranger in a strange land" necessitates negotiations of social boundaries with which one may have partial familiarity at best. What one living in diaspora thinks of oneself is only one component of an ongoing debate about who and what one is. Other components include the opinions of those fellow travelers with whom one experiences displacement, of those in the homeland to which one belongs, and of the residents in the locales in which one living in dispersion is now resident. These negotiations are emotionally freighted and are frequently marked by bidirectional assimilation across porous and permeable cultural boundaries. The experience of living in diaspora can also lead to conscious separation, misunderstanding, and acrimony. Within the Africana world, the tragic passing of both Whitney Houston and Trayvon Martin illustrates the aforementioned dynamics.

Houston's untimely death and the killing of Martin are both indicative of life in the African Diaspora, of the adaptive strategies used by Africana peoples to make sense of life and to resist forces that dehumanize and exploit people in twenty-first-century America. (Coverage of both events, and their aftermath, has been ubiquitous.) The former was an artist, troubled and to some extent misunderstood by her own community. The latter was a young man slain in part because he was viewed as a Black body out of place, a shadowy figure clothed in attire that appears to have identified him as suspicious and potentially dangerous. Consequently, a voice—"*the* Voice," in the minds of some commentators—and "the hoodie" are images of the promise, the possibilities, the adaptive strategies, and the theme of resistance that recur in the Black Diaspora.

Houston joins a long list of Black performers whose work crossed genres and cultural boundaries. She is also now part of a shorter list of artists, including the late Jimi Hendrix and Michael Jackson, who experienced significant personal turmoil as part of their own diasporas within the African American community itself. Her funeral displayed the intricate texture of Africana life, as well as the implicit dangers of being a child of the Black Diaspora. It also made clear the vital, yet extremely difficult role that artists frequently play in the unfolding drama of day-to-day existence in the Atlantic World (that is, the Americas and the Caribbean). To date, the case involving Martin's accused assailant has yet to be resolved. Even when it is, all of the details of what transpired on the night of his shooting may never be known. The tragedy is part of an extensive litany of incidents involving Africana women and men whose skin color, phenotypic traits, attire, political beliefs, and/or presence in a particular location have placed them in harm's way. The murder of Emmett Till, the arrest of Rosa Parks, the murder of Maurice Bishop, and the savage beating of Rodney King are just a few other examples that have been seared into the Black-Diasporan imaginary.

Houston and Martin also offer an interesting point of entry into the discussion of the poetics of social dislocation and insurgence in Black life and in ancient Israel. The former's music and public image propelled her beyond the limitations of the genres of soul and rhythm and blues and made it possible for her to transcend the at-times-hermetically-sealed categories into which the commercial music industry has often placed Black artists. Hers was, in a sense, a career built through deconstructive assimilation, that is, by the simultaneous embrace and dismantling of the ethos and norms of a dominant and pervasive culture of American artistic expression within which Africana genius tends to be construed in narrow and pejorative ways. That she is now remembered as an American musical icon, rather than one whose oeuvre can be defined simply by race or genre, is significant. This achievement did not come without great personal cost. She was fully embraced by neither her community of origin nor all in the general public. Her battles with addiction were public and the crises within her immediate family well known. She was a victim of overlapping displacements: racial, professional, familial, economic, and emotional. The battle to overcome them—at times successfully waged, at others not—ultimately claimed her life. That story, chronicled in her music and performances, is nonetheless a memoir of resistance and overcoming in the North American Diaspora. As for the latter, Trayvon Martin, his hooded sweatshirt has become a poignant trope of resistance to the racial profiling and violence that peoples of African descent have continued to suffer in this country at the hands of police and private citizens. With his death, the hoodie became emblematic of both resistance and eschatological convergence: a sign of defiance and a symbol of communal solidarity against hatred and ignorance. It is, in itself, a text that speaks *to* and *of* liberation.

As a group, early Hebrew poems speak of the challenges of diaspora in ways that are strangely reminiscent of "the Voice" and the hoodie. One can see manifest in them some of the realities that typify diasporan life, such as pressure to adapt and assimilate. One also finds in places a concomitant impulse to resist, or at least to challenge the privilege of, established orthodoxies. Other dynamics of diasporan life in general are also in evidence. For example, one detects in the corpus evidence of disparate social groups forging a collective identity while struggling to maintain their uniqueness (Genesis 49; Deuteronomy 33); ancestral traditions, particularly those relating to communal origins, being codified and curated (Exodus 15; Deuteronomy 32; 2 Samuel 22; Psalm 18; Psalm 78); the adaptation and inversion of indigenous and externally appropriated legend and lore (Psalms 29, 68); resistance strategies being negotiated and tested (Judges 5); the costs and benefits of cultural exchange and assimilation being contemplated (Numbers 23–24); the fate of women, the poor, and others on the social margins being pondered (1 Samuel 2); the tragic dimensions of intergroup strife being debated (2 Samuel 1); and the relationship between centralized forms of governance and the social welfare of communities in transition being considered (Psalm 72).

Some of these poems are unapologetic in their opposition to political hegemonies that foment diasporas (such as Exodus 15 and Judges 5) and are corrosive of human dignity. They are, in their bluntness, the literary equivalent of a poster featuring the Miami Heat basketball team garbed in hoodies as a sign of solidarity with Trayvon Martin.

Other poems deftly engage and subtly transmute motifs well known from the mythological lore of Canaan and the cultural milieu of early Israel's socially diverse mélange (Exod. 12:38). In so doing, poems such as 1 Samuel 2 and 2 Samuel 1 are not at all unlike the ballads of Whitney Houston: haunting in their beauty, depth, and poignancy. In the case of 2 Samuel 1—David's extraordinary lament over Jonathan's untimely demise—one is reminded of the sheer power of the refrain in Houston's now-classic rendition of the song "I Will Always Love You" and her equally stirring performance of "I Have Nothing." The hoodie and the Voice represent two complementary, though at times descanting, discourses of resistance within an Africana diaspora with historic roots and an evolving global presence. Early Hebrew poems contain comparable voices whose harmonies and discordant tones echo a Diasporan landscape equally complex. Linguistic evidence has led some to conclude that they are quite ancient. Internally, they deal with themes and events in Israel's formative years. Framing devices and placement suggest that the editors of the Tanak found several of them to be of such importance that they should be strategically placed within narratives and other collections of verse so as to highlight them. Many—such as Exodus 15, Deuteronomy 32, Judges 5, and Psalm 68—are disjunctive. They disrupt the aesthetic of their textual surroundings in much the same way that Houston's vocal style challenged the normative orthodoxies of the rock, rhythm and blues, and soul music continuum; and in the way that hoodies problematize popular notions of race, class, and identity. They force one to deal with bodies—literary, social, artistic, Black, straight, lesbian, gay, transgender, and questioning—perceived by those with the power to inscribe impermeable boundaries as being out of place. They make clear by their hypervisibility that they are exactly where they should be. Israel's most ancient bards, Whitney, and Trayvon have all passed from history. The poems, the Voice, and the shirt with the protective hood remain, enshrined in canons and memories that can neither frame nor tame their capacity to inspire and to liberate.

PART II

Early Hebrew Poems: A Compendium of Africana Readings

3

Zora Neale and the Lawgiver in Conversation

Exodus 15 and Moses: Man of the Mountain

EXODUS 15

1.

At that time Moses and the Israelites
Sang this song about YHWH.
Here are the words:

Let me sing to *Jah*.[1]
He is highly exalted.
He cast horse and horseman
Into the sea.

2.

My power is in *Jah's* song.
Surely, He is my salvation.
He is indeed my god.
That is why I praise him.
He is my ancestral god.
Therefore, I extol him.

3-4.

YHWH is a warrior.
Yes, *Jah* is his name!
As for Pharaoh's chariotry
And mighty men,

He hurled them into the sea.
Pharaoh's select officers
Have sunk into *Yam Suph*.

———
5.
The abyss covered them.
They descended to the depths like a stone.

———
6-7.
Your right hand, O *Jah*, is my glory.
With the strength of your right hand,
O *Jah*, you obliterated the enemy.
You destroyed your opponents
With your majestic presence.
You sent forth your anger
And consumed them like stubble.

———
7-8.
Yes, with wind from your nostrils
The waters piled up,
Stood like a flowing heap.
They became a mass
In the middle of the ocean.

———
9.
The enemy said:
"I will pursue, overtake, and divide plunder.
My soul will be full
I will unsheathe my sword,
My hand will dispossess."

———
10.
You blew with your wind.
The sea covered them.
They sank like a lead weight
In turbulent waters.

———
11.
Who is like you among the deities, O *Jah*?

Who is comparable?
Gloriously holy?
Fearfully praised?
A wonder worker?

———
12-13.
You extended your hand.
The earth swallowed them.
You led this people with your faithfulness,
You redeemed and guided them with power
To your sacred home.

———
14-15.
The peoples heard and trembled,
Agony gripped the Philistines.
Then the chiefs of Edom melted,
Trembling took hold of the Moab's rulers,
All the Canaanites melted.

———
16.
Fear and dread fell upon them
Because of your Arm's incredible strength.
They were dumb as a stone
Until your people crossed, O *Jah*,
While this people you created made safe passage.

———
17-18.
You brought and planted them on your ancestral mountain,
The dwelling place you yourself constructed, O YHWH,
The sanctuary, O *Jah,*
That your very hands built.
May YHWH reign forever and ever!

Rightly regarded as a linchpin of early Israel's self-conception, Exodus 15, known as the Song of the Sea, is accorded pride of place by many within the corpus of early biblical poems. Its celebration of freedom from tyranny and recall of miraculous rescue are hauntingly juxtaposed with images of mythological and earthly carnage as Yah, the Divine Warrior, marches forth to do battle. Clearly, such language must have evoked awe and a turn toward the contemplative among those twelfth-century BCE audiences that first heard it. It must certainly have had a comparable impact on those who preserved and folded it into the narrative structure of the Pentateuch.

Reading Exodus 15 through Zora Neale Hurston's *Moses: Man of the Mountain* (1939), one can't help but wonder about the poem, the one given credit in the narrative for having been the *mestre*[2] of the community that first gave voice to it, and the woman who reportedly led the singing of its antiphonal response. This is a relationship that Cross and Freedman pondered, ultimately associating it primarily with Miriam.[3] Hurston's imaginative retelling of the Moses story and the place Miriam occupies within it present a compelling *griosh* for engaging Exodus 15 and the complexities of twenty-first-century Africana life.[4]

In many respects, Hurston's tale is as much about the fashioning of the myth of a Hebrew savior embedded in the corridors of power by a frightened Hebrew child, as it is about the man who ultimately became the living embodiment of that tale. If Moses is envisioned in the novel as living legend, it is Miriam who helps create that legend. If Israel's liberation from Egypt is cast in the light of Moses' growing prowess as conjurer, part of this larger saga is Miriam's struggle for recognition in her family and among her peers. At the conclusion of his life, Moses stands atop Mount Nebo, and readers are told:

> The moon in its reddest mood became to him a standing place for his feet and the sky ran down so close to gaze on Moses that the seven great suns of the Universe went wheeling around his head. He stood in the bosom of thunder and the zig-zag lightning above him joined the muttering thunder. Fire and flame played all over the peak where the people could see. The voice of the thunder leaped from peak to plain and Moses stood in the midst of it and said "Farewell." Then he turned with a firm tread and descended the other side of the mountain and headed back over the years.[5]

Of Miriam's last days, Hurston's portrait is far less glorious. Psychically tormented by Moses' hand, which has "light in front of it and darkness behind" (262) because of her opposition to his Ethiopian wife, she is forced to acquiesce to the great leader's control over her life and her death. A woman of strength—indeed, a "two-headed woman with power" (135)—she is forced to acknowledge his superiority in order to die:

You see, I was a prophetess back in Egypt and I had power, that is what the people told me, anyhow. So when you didn't do to suit me, I made up my mind to fight your power with mine. But I found out I was no more against you than a grain of sand against a mountain, because you beat me and then you bottled me up inside my own body and you been keeping me in jail inside myself ever since. Turn me loose, Moses, so I can go and die (263).

Miriam *reads* Moses and speaks truth to his unrivaled power about his cruelty to her, his purported divinity, and his questionable ancestry. In her doing so, his control of her is relinquished. On her way back to her tent, her gait is said to have changed and "she seemed to see something with her eyes" (265). The next morning, she was dead. Her confrontation with Moses and her demise lead Moses to ponder the cost of Miriam's calling:

She had been sent on a mission as he had been sent, and the burden had torn and twisted her. She had been petty, envious and mean, but she had served. But then fate had provided no compensations for making her a bearer. Miriam had lived on hopes where other women lived on memories. And that was bound to do something to her. She was not sent to be what she wanted to be, so she had wasted herself procuring pangs for people who had" (264). It also forces Moses to acknowledge his debt, and that of the community, to a "patriot" with a "loveless life with one end sunk in slavery and the other twisted and snarled in freedom (265).

Within Israel's most ancient poems and the editorial comments that introduce them, Moses is mentioned four times (Exod. 15:1; Deut. 31:30, 33:1, and 33:4). The name of Miriam is completely absent from the tradition. Her only connection to the Song of the Sea is as prophet, sister of Aaron, and antiphonal respondent to a masterpiece already performed (Exod. 15:21). Hurston challenges this biblical marginalization of Miriam's role and offers a vision of the song's origin that places her at the center of it. It is her question to those assembled, "Didn't we outdo old Pharaoh, though?" (193), that generates a series of choral responses (from Aaron and others) and a communal dance that celebrate the victory. Once that performance is ended, Miriam leads a group of women in the extemporaneous composition and singing of yet another song (193–94). Thus, she is cast as the muse igniting early Israel's poetic fires. As for the Song of the Sea, Hurston seems to suggest that it belongs to no single poet; it belongs to the people. It is, to draw on the imaginary universe of Ishmael

Reed, a manifestation of "Jes Grew."[6] As for Miriam, she is the one whose prescient question conjures it.

Thus, Hurston weighs in authoritatively on the ultimate source of inspiration in the newly liberated community. When all is said and done, Miriam is the true catalyst. Her *call* (question), along with the community's embodied *response* through dance, creates the poem memorializing the miraculous victory over Egypt at the Yam Suph. Moreover, she offers a sobering look at Moses. Scholar, freedom fighter, mystic, religious innovator, murderer, root worker, he is a hero created in part by circumstance. His knowledge and skills are by-products of the privilege that accrues to him because of his gender, citizenship, social status, ambiguous ancestry, exile, and timely interventions by Miriam, who is a woman of power without recognized pedigree. By contrast, Miriam is the authentic maker, in some sense the true freedom fighter. Although Moses calls her a "patriot," she is much more than that. In Hurston's universe, she is the bridge between the old world and the new. Hers is a profound skepticism about the freedom and the world Moses represents. He is an opportunistic adept knowledgeable of Egyptian and Kenite wisdom, having gained aptitudes that outdistanced those of even his father-in-law, the great priest Jethro (117). She has acquired a substantial following through her ability to "hit a straight lick with a crooked stick" (135), but she is not a nation builder. Instead, the Song of the Sea and, indeed, Moses himself are her poems, her made things.

With this background in mind, it is hard to read Exodus 15 with an eye exclusively toward its prosody, the Canaanite motifs it contains, or the historical events that may have given rise to it. Instead, one's attention turns most naturally to the social dynamics to which the song might point. These could range from the dissolution of Egyptian political power in the late Bronze Age, to the peculiar realities that might lead the women in oppressed and newly constituted highland villages in Judea to create hymns that celebrate the emergence of a deity whose chief stewards and spokespersons will eventually relegate their (the women's) concerns to the margin and mute their voices. Hurston urges all who engage these poems to query their origins and the motives of those who may have written them, to ponder not just Moses, man of the mountain, but Miriam, prophetess of the people. She challenges readers to ponder how biblical texts in which the voices of women are silenced may be read—indeed, must be read—in ways that let us see, hear, and touch them.

If Exodus 15 is to be part of a twenty-first-century theological project aimed at creating communities of conscience within and beyond the Africana world that resist and dismantle exploitative institutional structures, then one has to pose "indecent" questions to and about it. Who are the power brokers for this YHWH? What of the wives and children of the Egyptians he has drowned? What of those who still, for whatever reasons, honor other *'ĕlîm* (deities)? Is this YHWH humble enough, sufficiently inclusive in his thinking, to allow women and men to neither acknowledge nor worship him? What of the indigenous peoples said to live in abject fear because of his steady advance? What is to be their fate? What is the story they will tell? Will they be alive to tell it? What will their poems recount? As for the ancestral mountain and the eternal reign, will the former be a sign of hope? Will the latter usher in a time of peace?

As for the modern realities to which these ancient signs may be seen to allude by readers today, have they the innate capacity to foster the kind of resistance that plants seeds of love, that nurtures the offspring of Miriam here and now? The jury is out. Time will tell.

Notes

1. In translating the divine name here and elsewhere in the early Hebrew poetic corpus, I have alternated between the nonvocalized representation of the Tetragrammaton and the abbreviated form of the divine name encountered numerous times in the Hebrew Bible, *yah*. The vocalization of the latter (i.e., *Jah*) intentionally reflects a pronunciation popular for some time in various locales within the Africana world, derived in part from Rastafarian colloquial usage and Reggae music. The choice, albeit an unusual one, reflects a conscious effort to bring these biblical poems into more direct conversation with contemporary Africana music that articulates spiritualties of resistance that unapologetically deploy symbolism from Africa and the Black Diaspora. Two excellent examples of songs that do so, and use *Jah* as the vocalization of choice for the divine name, are The Neville Brothers' "My Blood," track 1 on their CD *Yellow Moon* (UMG Recordings, 1989); and Third World's version of the song (written by Stevie Wonder and Melody McCully) "Try Jah Love," track 6 on the second disc of their CD *Reggae Ambassadors* (The Island Def Jam Music Group, 1993).

2. Portuguese for "master." This is a term often given to a master teacher of the Afro-Brazilian martial art known as Capoeira. As is the case in other martial arts, the master teacher is a numinous figure of sorts. I use the term here intentionally to call attention to Moses as warrior and liminal figure.

3. Frank Moore Cross and David Noel Freedman, *Studies in Ancient Yahwistic Poetry*, 2nd ed., Biblical Resource Series (Grand Rapids, MI: Eerdmans, 1997), 31.

4. I borrow the term *griosh*, which refers to a uniquely Africana method of interpretive engagement that incorporates the work of the African griot and the silence of the hush arbor, from Barbara Holmes, *Joy Unspeakable: Contemplative Practices of the Black Church* (Minneapolis: Fortress Press, 2004), 120.

5. Zora Neale Hurston, *Moses, Man of the Mountain* (1939; repr., New York: HarperPerennial, 1991), 288. Subsequent citations of this source will appear parenthetically in the text.

6. Ishmael Reed, *Mumbo Jumbo* (1972; repr., New York: Scribner, 1996), 6.

4

The Song of Deborah
Harriet, Ben, Jael, and "Jah Work"

JUDGES 5
1.
And Deborah sang on that day
With Baraq son of Abinoam
These very words:

———

2-3.
When *dreads*[1] were customary in Israel,
When folk had backbone—praise *Jah*;
Pay attention, Kings!
Rulers: listen!
I will sing of *Jah*,
And make music for *Jah*,
Israel's god.

———

4-5.
Jah, when you left Seir,
When you marched from Edom,
Earth shook,
Heaven dripped,
The thresholds poured forth water.
The mountains flowed
In the presence of *Jah*: Sinai's god,
Before *Jah*: Israel's Ruler.

———

6-7.

In the days of Shamgar the Anathite,
In the time of Jael,
Journeys stopped,
Travel was perilous.
Daily life ceased
Until I—Deborah—took a stand,
And asserted myself as Mother of Israel.

———

8.

Some chose new gods.
Then war broke out in the city gates,
But neither shield nor spear
Was seen among Israel's Forty Thousand.

———

9-10.

My heart was with Israel's leaders,
With the citizen volunteers—praise *Jah*.
Consider this, White Donkey Riders,
You who sit on wide garments
And travel along the way.

———

11.

Amid the sound of archers
At the watering places,
They recount the righteous deeds of *Jah*,
The exploits of his Israelite militia,
Then the people of *Jah*
Went down to city gates.

———

12.

Awake, awake, O Deborah!
"Get up, stand up," sing your song!
"Stand up, get up," lightning!
Take your captives, Abinoam's son.

———

13-14.

At that time a surviving remnant
Came to the nobility of *Jah*'s folk:

Came down to me, among the mighty ones.
From Ephraim (of Amalekite origin);
From you as well, O Benjamin,
From among your own people;
From Machir as well.
Those who bear the "administrator's staff"
Came down from Zebulun.

———

15-16.
My princes from Issachar
Were with Deborah—yea, faithful Issachar.
Baraq was sent into the valley behind him!
But among the divisions of Reuben
There were great misgivings.
Why did you stay in the sheep folds,
Listening to the hissing of flocks?
Within Reuben's clans
There were major reservations!

———

17.
Gilead settled across the Jordan.
As for you, Dan:
Why did you remain on your ships?
Asher stayed at the seashore,
Encamped by his mooring places!

———

18.
As for Zebulun—he gave up his soul to die,
But Naphtali was on the high ground as well.

———

19-21.
Kings came and made war;
Indeed, Canaanite kings fought
at Tanach by Megiddo's waters,
but they took no war booty.
The very stars fought from the heavens,
Fought with Sisera's host
From their celestial stations.

The Wadi Kishon washed them away,
the Wadi of Olden Days,
the Wadi Kishon.
Tell the story, O my soul!

———
22.

Then they smote their mighty warriors;
Indeed, gave them a thorough thrashing.[2]

———
23.

"Cursed be Meroz," says *Jah's* messenger.
"Thoroughly cursed be its inhabitants,
Because they did not come to *Jah's* aid,
To the assistance of *Jah* with other warriors."

———
24-26.

Most blessed among women be Jael,
Wife of Heber the Kenite,
Most blessed among nomadic women.
He asked for water,
She gave milk.
In a big bowl,
She presented ghee.
She put her hand to a tent peg,
Her right hand to a hammer of workmen.
She "hammered" Sisera,
Smashed his head,
Shattered and pierced his temple.

———
27.

He sank—fell between her feet.
He slept between her legs,
He sank and fell;
Where he sank,
There he fell,
Devastated!

———
28.

Behind a window,

Sisera's mother looks and cries.
Behind her lattice,
She wonders:
"Why is his mount ashamed to return?
Why do the sounds of his chariots delay?"

———

29–30.
Her wise princesses counsel her.
She tells herself,
"Surely he'll come back.
Have they not found and divided war spoil?
One or two women a head?
Booty and cloth for Sisera?
Plunder and much cloth?
Dyed cloth for the necks of the plunderers?"

———

31.
Thus, all your enemies
Perished, O *Jah*.
May those who love him
Be like the glorious sunrise.
As for the land,
It had rest for a generation.

It was almost impossible to grow up in Maryland and not know something about the American Revolution and the Civil War. Before leaving elementary, junior, and senior high school, we'd heard endless stories about the Lords Baltimore and Francis Scott Key. We'd been told of John Brown's raid and traveled to Harper's Ferry. We'd even learned about the Underground Railroad and one of its most famous conductors, Harriet Tubman. At least one of the station stops on that Freedom Train, Orchard Street African Methodist Episcopal Church, was well known within the community. Tubman herself was one of two Black Marylanders held up as role models for youth; the other was Benjamin Banneker. As a youngster in the 1950s and 1960s, I was very conscious of living in the shadow they cast. Both were exemplars of resistance: the former through escape (armed, if necessary), the latter by means of intellectual engagement. Pictures of Tubman have long reminded me of the tough and wizened African American women around whom I came of age. They were deaconesses and ushers at Sharon Baptist Church, where

I grew up. They served us meals in the cafeteria and taught our classes at Gilmore Elementary School. They were the neighbors next to whom many of us lived. They were the friends with whom our parents and grandparents socialized. They were our community's elders. Some of them, like my maternal grandmother and great-grandmother, had worked as domestics. For Black kids like me, Banneker's virtues were always held up for us to imitate: grace under pressure, perseverance, and unassuming industriousness, to name just a few. Tubman's tenacity and active resistance to oppression were presented to us as historical facts to be known rather than values to be emulated. However, it was hard not to internalize such traits, particularly if familial memories of racism and injustice were as acute as they were in our clan. Moreover, history shows clearly that the models of resistance exemplified by the lives of both Tubman and Banneker were pivotal in advancing the cause for freedom.

Many photographic images of Tubman are haunting. One, in particular, is remarkably reminiscent of photos I recall seeing in family albums and on fireplace mantels.[3] There is not the least hint in it that she was very much at home in the outdoors, had a finely tuned "sixth sense," worked as a scout and tactician for the Union Army, was a suffragette, or led between sixty-six and seventy-seven enslaved Africans out of bondage to freedom.[4] The pose, the domestic setting, the outwardly calm demeanor—all mask a steely resolve not unlike that I had come to know in the older Black women in my family and in those in the community who were the "fictive kin" we affectionately called "Aunt" or "Godmother." There was a little Harriet in every older Black woman to whom I was close. More than a few had remarkable stories of resistance and overcoming to tell.

Tubman left behind neither a personal diary nor a memoir. What we know of her comes from a relatively modest collection of primary sources, most of which have been written or compiled by others, many of whom heard her personal accounts and reenactments of chapters in her life. In the most significant biography on her to date, Jean Humez notes how such encounters "initiated the collaborative creation of a larger-than-life symbol of female heroism in resistance to the oppression of slavery and racism."[5] Although Humez's bringing together of 121 "stories and sayings" and 64 "documents" allows one to have more direct access to Tubman as a person, much about her continues to remain veiled even in these sources, inseparable at this point from the lore recorded about her. The flesh-and-blood woman has given way to what Humez so aptly terms "the Tubman legend."[6]

The same is true of two women encountered in Judges 5: Deborah and Jael. Both are remembered as freedom fighters. In fact, the song of the former celebrates, in part, the victory of the latter. For neither do we have more than a handful of biblical references. Like many other female figures in the Bible, textual references at once poignant and laconic must serve as the starting points for reimagining and breathing life into them. They are virtually inseparable from the poem in which their most memorable exploits have been preserved. The language of myth subsumes their flesh, blood, and spirits. It makes them concrete and accessible, particularly to those far removed from settings in which armed resistance to dehumanizing power structures is normative and expected. It "tames" them in much the same way that Tubman's photograph mutes her strength. However, the backstories to which Deborah's song and Harriet's stoic visage point prevent any of these women from being totally domesticated.

Among the artifacts left behind by Banneker were his commonplace book, his almanacs, and an assortment of writings. Together, they call to mind two universes of discourse central to his life: one scientific, the other esoteric. Banneker's almanacs, empirical studies, inventions, and occasional writings constitute an oeuvre oriented toward liberation. His response to the oppressive colonial environment of Maryland was the demonstration of Africana exceptionalism through research and entrepreneurialism. The life of the mind was his chosen arena for engagement. His quiet and relatively unassuming intellectual insurgency was comparable to the armed resistance of Tubman. Both were well known, yet they can be said to have done their most important work either indirectly or completely underground.

Two of Banneker's most poignant pieces of writing are a personal letter written to Thomas Jefferson in 1791 and a fragment of poetry written in the same year. In the first, he appeals to the then secretary of state to look with compassion on the "state of tyrannical thraldom, and inhuman captivity" suffered by those of African descent.[7] Banneker brilliantly lauds Jefferson's reasonableness and bases his call for human equality on the kinship all humans derive from common divine parentage. As for liberty, he grounds his appeal in our common nature and the obligations implicit in the Christian faith. He boldly calls attention to the tyranny from which the new republic had freed itself through revolution. He also cites the freedom derived from "the Supreme Ruler of the universe" (161) and affirmed by the American Declaration of Independence as a right that should be universally enjoyed, and encourages Jefferson and others to eschew their prejudices and allow "kindness and benevolence" to govern their interactions with his African "brethren" (162). In this same year, Banneker penned a scathing critique of America's exploitation of Africa and its peoples. The terse octet is a call to action for Christians:

Behold ye Christians! And in pity see
Those Afric sons which Nature formed free;
Behold them in a fruitful country blest,
Of Nature's bounties see them rich possest,
Behold them herefrom torn by cruel force,
And doomed to slavery without remorse,
This act, America, thy sons have known;
This cruel act, relentless they have done. (170)

The poem's accusatory invective is aimed at the church and at America as a whole, both of which are culpable for this crime. The theological charter for the former cannot possibly affirm that slavery hails from what Banneker terms, in his letter to Jefferson, "that Being from whom proceedeth every good and perfect gift" (161). Neither is it consistent with the ideals articulated in its foundational creeds. The letter to Jefferson and this poem are tools with which Banneker sought to deconstruct the political and religious underpinnings of slavery.

The Africana saga in the Atlantic World is replete with tales of freedom fighters, rebels, and escapees from slavery who worked overtly and covertly to dismantle the transatlantic slave trade bit by bit. The many successful and failed slave uprisings in the Americas and the Caribbean, as well as the actions of Toussaint-Louverture, "Gullah" Jack Pritchard, Nat Turner, John Brown, Harriet Tubman, and countless other insurgents, are a cherished, if little extolled, part of Africana lore. This part of our legacy is, for some, far too "messy"—embarrassing, as it were—in an era when our strategies for the redress of social inequities do not encourage armed confrontation and bloodshed. The most visible icon of the African American struggle for equality, President Barak Obama, is more an embodiment of Banneker than he is of any of the more memorable insurgents of ages past. His dignified demeanor and calm in the conduct of affairs of state and in the face of withering attacks against his competence and loyalty are reminiscent of Banneker's legendary decorum. Tubman and Banneker can be said, therefore, to be part of a complex and multidimensional economy of liberative praxis that included Africana women and men in disparate life settings and endowed them with varying degrees of freedom. Their stories are part of an Atlantic World epic that began with the initial European contacts with the African continent and continues into the twenty-first century.

The stories of Tubman and Banneker unfold against a backdrop of colonial conversations about democracy and the value of Black bodies within it. The documentary evidence we have for these discussions and for Tubman's and Banneker's roles therein is not inconsiderable. We know they existed. We have primary artifacts and secondary evidence to substantiate this fact. We can reasonably surmise certain facts about their hopes, dreams, ideas, and activities from such data. Unfortunately, the evidence we have pales in comparison to that which we have for other early American luminaries, such as George Washington, Thomas Jefferson, and Benjamin Franklin. There remains, therefore, an air of mystery about Tubman and Banneker—one that ignites imaginative speculation about their passions and inner lives. Biographical information thus both conjures and mythologizes them; it bids us to consider more than just the particularities of their lives. It asks us to *read* them as value-laden lore, Africana morality tales that orient us to the challenges of today and tomorrow. As it does for Deborah and Jael, the passage of time enables us to recreate and converse with Tubman and Banneker endlessly through what they have made and left behind. Just as the messiness of the tribal confederacy and Jael's triumph over Sisera are part of the "mother wit" preserved for posterity in Deborah's song, Tubman's Freedom Train and Banneker's almanacs are living fragments of Africana lore that urge us to take up and continue the struggle they initiated. Both understood this as a sacred and noble enterprise. As their stories, and those of Deborah and Jael remind us, such efforts must be ongoing. One could well liken them to what songwriter Ben Harper calls "Jah Work," which he characterizes as a vocation that is difficult, tireless, and ultimately, "never done."[8] In the years ahead, readers must decide whether to undertake this labor and heed "the call" to which Harper refers—a summons through the mythopoeic language of folklore and history from Deborah, Jael, Harriet, and Benjamin—as have so many of our elders.

Notes

1. Here I use a shortened plural colloquial form of the term "dreadlock."

2. This is a very loose translation of the Hebrew intended to capture the contextual meaning of the idiomatic Hebrew in the Masoretic Text.

3. See the image at http://www.americaslibrary.gov/aa/tubman/aa_tubman_subj.html.

4. On these and other facts about Tubman, see Jean M. Humez, *Harriet Tubman: The Life and Life Stories* (Madison: University of Wisconsin Press, 2003).

5. Ibid., 194.

6. Ibid.

7. Benjamin Banneker, quoted in Silvio Bedini, *The Life of Benjamin Banneker: The First African-American Man of Science*, 2nd ed. (Baltimore: Maryland Historical Society, 1999), 161. Subsequent citations of this source will appear parenthetically in the text.

8. Ben Harper, "Jah Work," *The Will to Live* (Virgin Records America, compact disc, 1997).

The Destructive Power of the Almighty

Grenada, Ivan, Soufrière Hills, and Psalm 29

PSALM 29

1-2.

A Davidic *mizmor*

"Give it up" for *Jah,* immortals,

Ascribe honor and strength.

Offer the honor deserving of *the Name.*

Worship in the beautiful holy place.

———

3.

Jah's Voice dominates the waters.

The Glorious God thunders.

Jah controls the great waters.

———

4.

The Voice of *Jah* is mighty.

The Voice of *Jah* is majestic.

———

5-6.

The Voice of *Jah* shatters cedar trees.

Jah decimates Lebanon's cedars.

The majestic white mountain dances like a calf,

Sirion like a young ox.

———

7.

The Voice of *Jah* flashes fiery flames.

The Voice of *Jah* makes the desert writhe.

Jah causes travail in the sacred wilderness.

—
8-9.

The Voice of *Jah* induces labor among hinds.
The Voice of *Jah* strips the forest,
And throughout his Temple there is the cry: "Honor!"

—
10.

Jah is seated upon *Mabbul*: the Great Flood.
May He reign as King until eternity.
May He grant strength to his people.
May He bless them with peace.

There is a partial blindness to which some living today in the African Diaspora succumb, the causes of which are difficult to define. It has to do with the ability to see what transpires in those parts of the Black world outside of one's own. Before access to the Internet became widespread, this was understandable. One would have to rely, for the most part, on community news outlets and word of mouth to know what was happening in the lives of Black people living elsewhere in the global community. Unfortunately, neither of these media was capable of offering more than partial or episodic coverage. The World Wide Web has remedied this problem to some extent. Information about current events in Africa, the Caribbean, South America, and elsewhere is available from any number of digital sources. Nonetheless, an empathetic gaze that takes in the entirety of the Africana milieu has been, and continues to be, difficult at best to cultivate.

This narrowness of vision inhibits a true appreciation of the devastating impact that certain natural and political disasters have had, and continue to have, on peoples of African descent throughout the world. In the past two decades, I have been particularly troubled by three such events. Two focus on Grenada: the political turmoil that resulted in the death of Maurice Bishop, and the devastation of Hurricane Ivan. One occurred in Montserrat: the volcanic eruption that rendered half of that island uninhabitable. All three can be read as epiphanies of a power destructive and creative, a force not unlike the one Psalm 29 ponders and attempts to tame through verse. This becomes clear when we juxtapose that poem with some of Bishop's speeches; the poetic remembrances of Hurricane Ivan in *Gone but Not Forgotten*; and those of the Soufrière Hills eruption in *Montserrat on My Mind*.[1]

Maurice Bishop (1944–1983) is an enigmatic figure whose short-lived tenure as prime minister of Grenada was tumultuous and tragic. His primary and secondary education was received in the island's Catholic schools. He received his collegiate and legal training in England. He returned to Grenada to practice law in 1970 and was soon thereafter involved in reform movements aimed at addressing some of Grenada's long-standing economic problems and political corruption. He and his New Jewel Movement (NJM) came to power via a 1979 coup. Bishop and his NJM supporters, renamed the People's Revolutionary Government (PRG), ruled the country until torn apart by factionalism in 1983. Bishop was subsequently arrested and, after being liberated by supporters, executed by a military firing squad. On the heels of his death, the United States sent troops to occupy Grenada. It maintained a military presence there until 1985.[2]

A champion of the island's poor and downtrodden, Bishop is, for many, both hero and martyr. This is not surprising, given NJM's 1976 platform calling for democracy, human development, accessible health care, cultural advancement, local control of natural resources, full employment, a reasonable living standard for everyone, freedom of speech and religious expression, universal liberation for the oppressed, and social unity and transformation.[3] The platform was perceived by some as a much-needed change from both colonial rule by the British and the policies of ousted prime minister Eric Gairy (1922–1997). Bishop understood well that his policies would have powerful detractors in the United States and among its international allies. In a speech honoring the third anniversary of the Grenadian Revolution, he offered a compelling vision of its outcomes:

> Our detractors and villifiers [sic] have neutron bombs and wage chemical warfare. We hold the truth of our process out towards them: our free health, our free education, our free school books and uniforms, our free milk, our national bus service, our international airport, our clinics, our fishing fleet and saltfish plant, our agro-industries, our house repair program, our Centres for Popular Education. These are the great truths of the Grenada revolution.[4]

On an island rich in resources, many of Grenada's citizens lived in abject poverty. The reforms advocated by NJM/PRG began a political storm whose metaphorical winds began to dismantle what many perceived to be a repressive political and economic status quo.

At stake, ultimately, was the issue of where the power to rule should ultimately reside. For Gairy, at least late in his regime, it was de facto, if not de jure, sole rule; he is said to have claimed divine authority for his power.[5] For Bernard Coard, Bishop's one-time friend, who arrested Bishop and sanctioned his murder, it was perhaps shared governance with Bishop.[6] For Bishop himself, it was—at least in theory—the people of Grenada. The tragedy that claimed his life suggests that it was perhaps chaos that ruled, a turmoil that permanently removed Gairy from office, resulted in Coard's imprisonment and humiliation, and claimed Bishop's life.

Hurricane Ivan plays a curious role in this tragic saga. When it swept through the Caribbean, in 2004, it claimed the lives of many and brought indescribable devastation to Grenada. One poet, Serajul Hack, recalls the havoc it wrought:

Hurricane conjures dark romantic images . . .
Of raging seas:
Trees . . . everywhere flattened . . .
Fresh upturned . . . tree roots . . .
The howling . . . overhead . . .
Houses . . . blown to shreds . . .
Twisted corrugated . . .
Galvanized sheets,
And, not to mention,
death and destruction![7]

One of the structures "blown to shreds" was the island's Richmond Hill Prison. Storm winds created several breaches in its walls, thereby allowing some prisoners to escape. Coard, one of its most famous inmates, elected not to flee either the remaining years of his punishment or the wrath of Ivan. The rebuilding after Ivan; the passing of Gairy, in 2007; and Coard's release from prison two years later mark, in some ways, the end of a tempestuous era in Grenada's history. In the summer of 2012, Grenadians celebrated the ascent of a new and far less controversial leader, this time in the realm of sport. Kirani James's victory in the 400-meter finals at the Thirtieth Olympiad in London 2012 marked the first time the country claimed an Olympic medal of any kind. A nineteen-year-old with a winning personality and a warm smile, is he the symbol of a new era in Grenada? Is his success emblematic of the kind of reign—of athletic competition and the commodification of Africana bodies—that will mark the end of the colonial and postcolonial storms that have destabilized Grenada and other countries in the Caribbean? Is this the kind of power able to control the unruly forces of politics and nature that have periodically engulfed the region? Are the prowess and advertising potential of a sprinter the new symbol of hope, of Jah's favor for Grenada?

What impact does any of this have on an African American born and raised in a city near the shores of the Chesapeake Bay—a locale that could be considered, relative to Grenada, in the "extreme north" (Ps. 48:2) of the known world? Growing up, I had little direct experience of the West Indies, save what I learned from one of my uncles, whose family was from St. Croix. Our city rarely knew extremes in weather. Hurricane season did not have the impact on the popular imagination that it did in places like Grenada. Other than the occasional thunderstorms that came our way, we had no immediate point of reference for any phenomenon that, in the words of Psalm 29, "shatters cedar trees" (v. 5), "causes travail" (v. 8), or "strips the forest" (v. 9). Our political storms were not rooted in attempts to free ourselves from British colonialism; they had more to do with the long-term effects of a Black population recovering from Maryland's peculiar brand of Jim Crow segregation. Our grade-school curriculum offered little in the way of exposure to the Africana world beyond the handful of great women and men of African descent that simply could not be ignored. The geopolitical complexities of the Caribbean and the cultural interdependence of Africana peoples living in Diaspora were not topics I recall discussing at great length. This educational lacuna would be partially filled for me years later, at Hampton Institute. Unfortunately, even at this legendary African American college, courses focusing directly on Africa and the Caribbean were few in number. It was not until my adult life that my exposure to and awareness of the Caribbean increased. This appreciation would deepen in 1984, while I sat in the undercroft of the Alexander Crummell Episcopal Church in the Detroit neighborhood of Highland Park and listened to members of the Black Nationalist community—poets and activists—talk in almost hushed tones about what was then transpiring in Grenada. Just shy of a decade later, I would have my one and only opportunity to walk the streets of Saint George's and its outlying environs, to witness firsthand how geopolitical forces, natural disasters, the inequitable distribution of wealth, and other factors have left their mark on Grenadian society; and how unprotected it has been against such maelstroms—as well as hurricanes such as Ivan—that lay waste dreams. In 1995, I would watch in horror as the Soufrière Volcano erupted on Montserrat, setting in motion a new Diaspora in the Lesser Antilles, the full impact of which will take years to determine.[8] Suffice it to say, such experiences cannot help but shape an Africana encounter with Psalm 29.

An old Phoenician hymn adapted for liturgical use in ancient Israel: there is much to support this now-classic interpretation by H. L. Ginsberg.[9] As for the psalm's date, the twelfth-century proposal offered by Freedman still seems plausible. Reading it as a semiotic construct, *apud* James Kennedy, is particularly intriguing. His closing remark raises interesting questions about the psalm's backstory:

> As the psalm concludes, the reader may envision Israel's representatives to the divine assembly, who are as much the object of address in vv. 1Ab, B and 2 as are $b^e n\hat{e}$ *'ĕlîm* [immortals], as being acutely, frightfully, but hopefully aware that $q\hat{o}l$ *YHWH* [voice of YHWH] can protect the nation or toss it from the surface of the earth.[10]

Might one see here sentiment that runs counter to that of Deuteronomic theology and its covenantal conception of the deity? Does Psalm 29 resonate with a theophany like Job 38? Is acknowledgment of the power of the divine voice the *only* choice humans ultimately possess when confronted with a force that can heal or harm, save or destroy? Are the only potential responses silence or the proclamation, "Honor!"? Would the former amount to tacit rejection of the deity's sovereignty? Does the latter offer *guaranteed* protection in the face of cataclysm? These queries are in themselves discomfiting. That this psalm offers no clear answers is equally disquieting, as disquieting as Maurice Bishop's death, Ivan's wrath, and Soufrière Volcano's rendering of some 50 percent of Montserrat uninhabitable.

Perhaps we would do well to keep in mind that the experiential dimensions of the Black Diaspora, such as the palpable impact of social and personal fragmentation and the persistent crises that emerge as individuals and social groups seek to deal with it, generate thinking that is oriented toward final outcomes. Thus, one can speak of there existing a concept of a teleological or eschatological diaspora within the Africana imaginary. Perhaps it is this reality toward which those experiencing crisis "press on" (Philippians 3:12, 14, NRSV), to draw on a well-worn Pauline trope, and on which Africana peoples call when they seek to make sense of natural disasters; when they recall the Grenadian Revolution or Hurricane Ivan; or when they try to reassemble the pieces of broken dreams and shattered hopes in their continuing struggle to survive storms, eruptions, and political upheavals.[11]

Notes

1. See Serajul Hack, *Gone . . But Not Forgotten . . . Hurricane Ivan* (Pittsburgh, PA: Dorrance, 2007); and Dorine S. O'Garro, *Montserrat on My Mind: Tales of Montserrat* (Bloomington: Author House, 2004).

2. This basic information comes from the biographical profile by Lisa Clayton Robinson, "Bishop, Maurice," in *Africana: The Encyclopedia of the African and African American Experience*, ed. J. Kwame Anthony Appiah and Henry Louis Gates Jr., 2nd ed. (New York: Oxford University Press, 2005).

3. Maurice Bishop, *Forward Ever!* (Sydney, Australia: Pathfinder, 1982), 23.

4. Ibid., 281.

5. Hugh O'Shaughnessy, "Sir Eric Gairy" (obituary), *Independent* (London), August 25, 1997, http://www.independent.co.uk/news/people/obituary-sir-eric-gairy-1247273.html.

6. Robinson, "Bishop, Maurice," 471; Jorge Heine, "The Return of Bernard Coard," *Gleaner* (Jamaica), http://jamaica-gleaner.com/gleaner/20090920/focus/focus6.html.

7. Hack, *Gone. . .*, 4.

8. O'Garro is an example of an author who deployed the Psalter (i.e., Psalm 121) in creative reflections on this event. See *Montserrat on My Mind*, 3–10.

9. H. L. Ginsberg, "A Phoenician Hymn in the Psalter" (1935), in *Atti del XIX Congresso Internazionale degli Orientalisti* (Rome: Bardi, 1938).

10. James M. Kennedy, "Psalm 29 as Semiotic System: A Linguistic Reading," *Journal of Hebrew Scriptures* 9, no. 12 (2009): 21.

11. I am deeply indebted to my colleague Dr. Leslie James of DePauw University for a series of ongoing conversations (personal and via electronic mail) about storms, Psalms, Diaspora, Grenada, and texts—both biblical and classical—that are engaged in Africana life.

6

_____

Playing "the Dozens" and Community Formation

Rethinking Genesis 49 and Deuteronomy 32–33

GENESIS 49

1-2.

Then Jacob started *sounding on* his sons as follows:
Gather round and let me tell you
What will happen to you in the days ahead.
Come. Pay attention, children of Jacob.
Listen closely to Israel, your Patriarch.

___

3-4.

Reuben, you are my firstborn,
My most powerful and strongest;
Matchless in honor and might;
Reckless like water,
You don't sit still.
Instead, you go up from your father's beds
And defile my couch.

___

He got up. . . .[1]

___

5-7.

Simeon and *Levi* are brothers.
Implements of war are their weapons.
Don't be party to their scheming, O my soul;
Neither join their cohort.

They kill people in anger
And hamstring oxen for pleasure.
Cursed be both their wrath—it is extensive;
Their fury—it is ravaging indeed.
I'll let them parcel shares in Jacob,
And scatter them in Israel.

―――

8-10.

Judah, your brothers praise you.
Your hand is on your adversaries' neck.
The sons of your father venerate you.
Judah is a lion's cub:
You go up from eating prey, my son.
He bows and coils like a lion.
Like a lion, who can stand up to him?
The scepter of rule will not leave Judah.
The authoritative decree will not leave his presence
Until Shiloh arrives.
To him belongs the obedience of the people.

―――

11-12.

Binding the donkey to the vine,
To a choice vine a young donkey,
He washes his clothing in wine,
In the blood of grapes his robe.
His eyes are redder than wine,
His teeth are whiter than milk.

―――

13.

Zebulun resides along the seacoast
By the ship-filled coastline,
And his farthest extent reaches Sidon.

―――

14-15.

Issachar is a strong donkey
Reclining between the Sheepfolds.
He saw that the resting place was good
And that the land was pleasant,
So he offered his shoulder to bear a load

And was subjected to forced labor.

———

16-17.

Dan judges his people
As one of Israel's tribes.
Dan will be a serpent upon the road,
A viper on the way,
Biting the horse's heel
So that its rider falls off to the rear.

———

18.

I wait patiently for your salvation, YHWH.

———

19.

As for *Gad*, a marauding band pursues him,
Yet he too pursues tenaciously.

———

20.

From *Asher* will come an abundance of food.
He will indeed provide fine things to the king.

———

21.

Naphtali is a wild doe,
One speaking beautiful words.

———

22.

Joseph is son of a fruitful vine,
Child of a fruitful vine by a spring.
Branches go out upon a wall.

———

23-24.

Some embittered him.
Indeed, archers shot and bore a grudge against him,
So his bow rests among the mighty,
And the arms of his hands are agile,
Because of the support of the *Mighty One of Jacob*,
Because of the *Name of the Shepherd—The Rock of Israel*.

25.

Because of *El, Your Father*—surely he will help you
And *Shaddai*—who blesses you.
Because of the blessings of the *Heavens* above,
By means of the blessings of the *Deep* stretched below,
Blessings of the *Eternal Mountains* and *Primordial Womb*.

26.

The blessings of your Father are stronger than
Those of *Horay*—at the border of the *Ancient Hills*
May they rest on the head of *Joseph*,
On that of his brother, the Nazir.

27.

Benjamin is a destructive wolf;
In the morning he eats prey,
And in the evening he divides plunder

DEUTERONOMY 32

Moses began *woofin'* in the presence of the entire Israelite assembly,
Using the words of this song, in their entirety:[2]

1.

Give ear, O Heavens, so I may speak.
Let Earth hear the words of my mouth.

2.

May my advice fall like raindrops,
Let my words drip like dew,
Like showers upon the grass,
Torrents on foliage.

3-4.

I will call upon the *Name of YHWH*,
Praise the greatness of our God.

The work of the *Divine Rock* is perfect,
Because all his ways are just.
El is the embodiment of faithfulness,
And there is no iniquity in him.
He is *Righteous* and *Upright*

―――

5.

As for his progeny, it is utterly perished.
He has no children.
They are polluted:
A generation impure and perverse.

―――

6.

Why do you repay YHWH in this way,
You foolish and unwise people?
Is not He your *Father*?
Isn't YHWH
The *One who Created and Established you*?

―――

7.

Remember the olden days,
Recall years in the distant past.
Ask your father—he will tell you;
Your elders—they will inform you.

―――

8-9.

When *Elyon—the Highest*—apportioned the nations,
When He subdivided humanity,
He fixed boundaries for the peoples
According to the number of celestial deities.
The sole inheritance of YHWH was his people;
Jacob was His designated progeny.

―――

10.

He found them in a desert land,
In the utter chaos of Jeshimon.
He attended to and watched over them,
As a cherished possession.

―――

11-12.

As an eagle rouses its nest of younglings
He flutters and stretches his wings.
He gathers and lifts them on his pinions.
YHWH alone leads them;
No foreign deity accompanies them.

13-14.

He makes them ride upon the high places
And eat the produce of the cultivated fields.[3]
They suck honey from *the Rock*
And oil from *the Flint Boulder,*
Cow's butter and sheep's milk
With the fat of lambs and rams from Bashan
And male goats with kidney fat
Wheat and wine—the blood of grapes—you will drink.

15-17.

Jeshurun grew immensely prosperous—fat, thick, and engorged.
He forgot the god who created him,
Neglected *the Rock* who saved him.
They made him jealous through strangers.
They made him angry by means of abominable actions.
They sacrificed to deities that were not (their) own,
Gods they did not know.
They embraced new traditions:
Things to which their ancestors did not adhere.

18.

You overlooked *the Rock* who bore you,
Forgot *God who Gives Birth*

19.

YHWH saw this and spurned them
Out of anger toward his sons and daughters.

20.

He said:
"Let me hide my face from them

And see what will become of them,
For they are a perverse generation;
Unfaithful offspring are among them.

—
21.

"They forsook me for nondeities,
Angered me with their vain deeds.
I will anger them by means of a nonpeople.
With a foolish nation I will infuriate them.

—
22.

"Fire will indeed blaze from my nose.
And burn to the depths of Sheol.
It will consume the land and its produce,
And consume the foundations of the mountains.

—
23-24.

"I overwhelm them with calamities.
My arrows will demolish them,
As will the wasting effects of hunger,
The consumptive plague,
And crawling things of the dust.

—
25-26.

"Outside, the sword will demolish them.
Inside, they will be terrified.
This will be true for the young man and maiden,
For the infant and the aged alike.
I purposed to obliterate and extinguish their memory
From the human family.

—
27.

"However, I feared external rebuke
And that our enemies might say:
"'It was our power that triumphed,
YHWH is not responsible for this.'

—
28-30.

"Alas, they are a people devoid of acuity,

Folk absent understanding.
After all, how could one person
Pursue a thousand adversaries,
Or two cause a myriad to flee,
If not at the behest of their *Rock,*
YHWH—*The One Who Buys and Sells Them?*

———

31.
"Recall, our *Rock* is not their *Pebble,*
Nor are our enemies our judges.

———

32-33.
"Theirs is the vine of Sodom.
Their grapes are from Gomorrah's vineyards:
Poisonous fruit,
Bitter clusters.
Their wine is serpents' venom,
The cruel bite of adders.

———

34-35.
"Am I not *He*—the *One Who Stored the Seal*
In My Treasury?
Vengeance and score settling are my responsibility;
In time their feet will grow unsteady
Because the Day of Edom draws near;
It comes quickly."

———

36.
Yes, YHWH will judge his own people,
And will bring comfort to his devotees,
Because he recognizes that their power is gone,
That their bondage and abandonment are finished.

———

37-38.
So He muses:
"Where are those gods, those *stones* who rescued them?
The ones who consumed the fat of their sacrifices
And drank the wine of their libations?
Let them stand up and assist them.

Let one of them serve as their secure place.

———
39.

"Be clear about this:
I alone am *the One.*
There is *no* other deity except me.
I kill and give life.
I wound and heal.
Only *my* power can rescue.

———
40–41.

"I raise my hand to the heavens
And say: 'To me alone belongs Eternal Life.'
I send lightning as my sword.
My hand directs all things with justice.
I repay my adversaries with vengeance,
And settle scores with those who hate me.

———
42.

"I make my arrows drunk with blood;
My sword consumes the flesh
From the blood of the defiled and captives
From the heads of long-haired enemies."

———
43.

Rejoice, O Nations, with his people,
Because he avenges the blood of his servants,
Brings vengeance to his adversaries,
And populates the land with his people.

DEUTERONOMY 33
1.

And this is the *blessing* with which Moses, man of God,
Graced the Israelite community before his death.

———
2.

He said:
YHWH came from Sinai,
Indeed, He arose from Seir,

And shone forth over them from Mount Paran.
There came with him a myriad of Holy Ones;
At his right hand was the flaming testimony.

___

3.

It is a certainty—he loves the populace!
All of his Holy Ones are at your disposal.
Indeed, they will follow close behind you.
He will lift your burdens.

___

4-5.

The Torah that Moses commanded us,
Is the inheritance of Jacob's assembly.
May there be a monarch in Jeshurun,
Among the gathering of the rulers of a unified people—Israel's tribes.

___

6.

Let *Reuben* live and not die;
May his men be a multitude!

___

7.

And he said this concerning *Judah*:
Hear, O YHWH, Judah's voice,
And return his power to his people.
He contends for himself,
So may you be a Support against his adversaries.

___

8.

And concerning *Levi* he said:
Your Thummim and Urim
Belong to your righteous men,
Whom you tested at Massa
And contended with at the waters of Meribah,

___

9-10.

Those who said to their fathers and mothers—I do not acknowledge you
And to their brothers—I recognize you not,
Who told their sons that they did not know them.

___

Because they preserved your words
And kept your covenant.
They passed on your judgments to Jacob,
And your torah to Israel.
They offered up incense before you
And whole offerings upon your altar.

_____

11.

Bless, O YHWH, his power;
May you accept the work of his hands.
Shatter the loins of his enemies and haters,
So they cannot stand.

_____

12.

Concerning *Benjamin* he said:
Beloved of YHWH:
May he dwell in safety.
May he be a Covering for him all day
And dwell between his shoulders.

13.

Concerning *Joseph* he said:
Blessed by YHWH is his Land,
By the choice gifts of the Heavens,
The dew the *Primordial Depths* extending beneath it,

_____

14.

The choice gifts of the harvest of the Sun,
The choice gifts of the produce of the Moon

_____

15.

The best of the Ancient Mountains,
The choice gifts of the Eternal Hills;

_____

16.

The choice gifts of Earth and its fullness,
The favor of the Bush Dweller:
May these things rest on the head of Joseph,
On the brow of the prince of his brothers.

17.

First-born of his strength,
Majesty belongs to him.
The horns of the *Divine Ox* are his horns.
With them he pushes the peoples
To the very ends of the earth.
These are the myriads of *Ephraim,*
The thousands of *Manasseh.*

18.

Regarding *Zebulun* he said:
Rejoice O *Zebulun* in your going out;
Indeed, do likewise, *Issachar,* in your tents.

19.

The peoples of the mountains cry out.
There they sacrifice righteous offerings,
For the abundance of the peoples they suck,
Things having been covered and hidden in the sand.

20.

Concerning *Gad* he said:
Blessed is the one expanding *Gad.*
Like a lion he sits.
He tears off arms and heads.

21.

He assays the best things as his own.
Indeed, there was found a once-concealed royal hoard;
He brought it out to the heads of the people.
He enacted the righteousness of YHWH;
His judgments are with Israel.

22.

Regarding *Dan* he said:
Dan is a lion's cub.
He leaps from Bashan.

23.
Of *Naphtali* he said:
Naphtali is sated with favor,
And full of YHWH's blessing.
Sea and Southland
May they inherit.

___

24.
Concerning *Asher* he said:
Blessed among sons is *Asher*,
Let him be one accepted among his brothers,
Who dips his feet in oil.

___

25.
Your bolts are iron and bronze.
May your days rival your strength.

___

26.
No one compares to the God of *Jeshurun*:
The *One Riding through the Heavens in Strength*,
Proudly traversing the clouds;

___

27.
The Habitation; *the Ancient God*;
The One beneath the Everlasting Arms.
May he drive your enemies from before you,
And may he say—Destroy!

___

28.
May Israel dwell securely, singly.
The *Eye of Jacob* is on the Earth;
May his Heavens drip grain, wine, and dew!

___

29.
Israel, you are indeed blessed.
Who is like you—a people saved by YHWH?
The Shield is your help, sword, and pride!
Your enemies will be perplexed;

But when it comes to you,
On high places you will tread.

As a kid, I hated playing "the dozens." Somehow, talking about people's parents, relatives, clothing, appearance, and personal lives in often outlandish and derogatory fashion struck me as disrespectful and mean-spirited. That kind of "loud talking" and "woofing" didn't sit well with me.[4] We didn't do that kind of thing at home. Neither my parents nor my grandparents approved of it. It didn't conform to standards of appropriate communication within a family or among friends. Other forms of interpersonal communication in which explicit and more subtle dimensions of the challenge, riposte, and imaginative verbal exchanges that Henry Louis Gates Jr. and others remind us typify Africana communication *were* present.[5] Such "signifying" might encompass humorous personal anecdotes shared during meals; jokes and friendly banter when doing yard work or household chores; impromptu updates on things going on with relatives while driving to visit them; or artful recountings of family members' misadventures. There were people in our family who were particularly gifted at this, those who could seemingly channel the spirit of the Yoruba trickster Esu at will.[6] However, in our clan, middle-class values inhibited the extent to which Gates's assertion that "learning how to Signify is often part of our adolescent education" was true.[7] Rather than helping to strengthen communal bonds and dissipate aggression, it was, I sensed, particularly among some of my childhood and adolescent mates, often a prelude to physical altercations. Thus, I always kept in the back of my mind that certain types of signifying were potentially dangerous and unpredictable. For example, on my block, if you couldn't fight, or run fast, the topic of mothers was generally off limits.

There was another dimension to playing "the dozens," "talking trash," or "shootin' the bull." It involved reading between the lines, that is, sensing when things were, as we used to say, "about to get ugly," that they had reached a critical point when the tone of the conversation was about to shift, or when some of the folk involved might be tired of talking or ready to disband. For someone like me—an only child living in a neighborhood where it seemed everyone had siblings; an asthmatic, unathletic, rather bookish kid whose hobbies consisted of, among other oddities, reading science fiction and model railroading—I didn't "hang out on the block" enough to become truly proficient. Maybe this was the real source of my aversion to it. I was far better at sensing the flow and keeping track of who was winning, losing, or "getting pissed" when people were "talking smack" to one another. Now and then, I might weigh in with a comment or two, but rarely, if ever, would I be a principal conversant. I was a teacher's kid, the nerd in the 'hood who spoke Standard English. I didn't have the "street cred" to be taken seriously if I tried to signify. I wasn't stupid enough to "fake the funk." I learned early on, though, that I had a kind of sixth sense. I could read body language: eye ticks, changes in breathing patterns, and even verbal intonations. I could feel, at times with frighteningly uncanny accuracy, the silences between gibes. I learned how to steer a verbal confrontation that was about to devolve into seriously hurt feelings or a fight by coming up with a stupid joke or an off-the-wall comment. I became an intuitive, a "signifying whisperer." That was an important skill to possess, particularly in an environment where young Africana men, and women established friendships, built coalitions, and secured their place in the social hierarchy by "breaking bad" when circumstances called for it. Knowing how to "read" dangerous situations, keep quiet when verbal confrontations were escalating, and escape when talking was about to cease and fists were about to fly were the competencies I refined early on. I'm reminded of this when I ponder some of the possible deeper meanings of texts like Genesis 49 and Deuteronomy 32 and 33, which strike me as signifying discourse.

So, what can be read between the lines of Jacob's "scoring" on his sons (Genesis 49)? What can be heard in the silences of Moses' "loud talking" about Israel (Deuteronomy 32)? What sort of "woofin'" was going on in his blessing of the tribes (Deuteronomy 33)? Who are the luminaries, sons, or tribal groups identified in these poems as the most proficient signifiers? Who are the ones most often on the receiving end of harsh critique? Who appear to be the most enigmatic—the "whisperers"—about whom the least is said? Jacob and Moses are cast, at least according to the rubrics introducing these poems, as the signifiers par excellence. If we count the oracular utterance embedded within Deuteronomy 32, we have to add YHWH to this list as well.

As for signifying itself, if one uses these particular pieces as exemplary of the practice, it consists of artful truth telling about those within Israel's communal matrix; ancestral reminiscences about tribes, deities, and YHWH; and theologically grounded praise and critique of a community's fidelity to its chosen god. On the surface, it has the appearance of being a carefully structured monologue placed on the lips of an ancient hero. This creates a considerable aura of authority and finality to what is said, a sense that what Jacob or Moses articulated about a tribe or an event in the past is canonical. However, the juxtaposition of voices, and even of signifying subgenres, suggests an ethos in which traditions about people, places, and events are understood to compete for "air time." Those who are "called out" for specific mention vary, as do the order in which they are noted and the amount of attention they receive. Furthermore, one can't help but wonder about the teleological objective of this kind of discourse in both its original setting and within the canonical framework of the Hebrew Bible.

In Genesis 49, Jacob the patriarch engages in some truth telling about his offspring. At the outset, due deference is given to Reuben's status as firstborn, physical prowess, and recklessness. A creative, indeed playful, reading of the passage dealing with him might involve seeing his father's frank assessment as a stimulus leading to his departure from the gathering with his siblings (v. 4). Cast as comparably dangerous are Simeon, Levi, Judah, Dan, Gad, and Benjamin. Of these, one—Judah—is singled out nonetheless as particularly well suited to govern. Zebulun is portrayed as an enigma, one about whom no critical comment is made. Equally mysterious are Naphtali, whose purported proficiency with words (v. 21) is intriguing, and Joseph, the articulation of whose virtues is without parallel in the text. Issachar is the least favorably presented of all the brothers, and Asher's value is measured in terms of his provision for royalty—perhaps an allusion to subservience to Judah. Within what might be termed an economy of signifying, the major contestants—those about whom much is known and can be said—are Reuben, Simeon, Levi, Judah, Dan, Gad, Benjamin, and Joseph. Those on the proverbial sidelines because of subjugation by or subservience to others are Issachar and Asher. The whisperers—best characterized as brokers whose power comes from their skill with words or their lack of geographical proximity—are, perhaps, Zebulun and Naphtali.

Deuteronomy 33, though of a similar genre, has an altogether different tone. It begins with a retelling of YHWH and his divine contingent's trek from Sinai and YHWH's devotion to his people (vv. 2-5) and concludes by calling attention to his incomparable power (vv. 26-29). It then proceeds with a series of blessings specific to the community's respective tribes. The length and tone of several appear to indicate the high esteem in which the author holds the group in question. This is particularly true of Levi and Joseph, both of whom receive substantial evocations for prosperity. By comparison, those blessings directed toward Reuben, Judah, Benjamin, Zebulun, Issachar, Dan, Naphtali, and Asher are brief indeed. The blessings of Reuben, Zebulun, Issachar, and Dan are by far the tersest. The wishes that Reuben simply "live" and grow numerous (v. 6); that the tribe of Zebulun "rejoice" in its "going out"; and that Issachar's does likewise within its "tents" (v. 18) perhaps mark all three as whisperers in this poem.

In Deuteronomy 32, Moses' song assumes cosmic dimensions. On one level, it presents a straightforward narration of the highs and lows of Israel's fraught relationship with its god, YHWH. Read with an eye toward the dynamics of woofin', it reveals another dimension. It shows how such discourse can serve to make present viscerally the voice and internal musings of the Celestial Signifier, that metaphorical "Rock" who possesses the power to "kill," "give life," "wound," or "heal" (v. 9). It demonstrates that there is a complementary relationship between signifying and another set of practices related to resistance, protection, healing, and wholeness at home in the Africana Diaspora of North America: conjuring. In this text, Moses' signifying and conjuring reveal one means through which those in need of divine help may receive it: through invoking *Jah*'s name (v. 3) and sobriquets. The latter include "Divine Rock" (v. 4), "Father" (v. 6), Elyon—"the Highest" (v. 8), "Rock" (v. 13), "the Flint Boulder" (v. 13), and others. Within early Israel and certain parts of the Africana world, appellations are bearers of power. To name, or know the name of, a thing is to understand, forge a relationship with, control, or exercise power over it. In light of Africana lore, therefore, it would appear that in Deuteronomy 32 one sees Moses, the signifying conjurer, opening a way to the one to whom "alone belongs Eternal Life" (v. 40).

Within the ecology of Africana life, there has long been a role for signifying, what I have termed whispering, and conjuring. If Esu and the "signifying monkey" are the embodiment of the first and the third, perhaps the Yoruba god Osain, the divine herbalist and possessor of esoteric knowledge, can be said to represent in some way the second.[8] He is said to have secret knowledge of plants with curative properties. His abode is the forest, the place that also served as home to the "hush arbors" where enslaved Africans in the South preserved and at times transformed indigenous worship traditions from their homelands. These practices constitute a threefold matrix of Africana liberative discourse and praxis oriented toward the building of community, truth telling, the amelioration of conflict, and the harnessing of esoteric power for protection and to foster wholeness. The ancient poems preserved in Genesis 49 and Deuteronomy 32–33 urge us to ponder two important questions: The first is how such a matrix might have worked in ancient Israel. The second is whether now might once again be a time when Africana spiritualities of resistance—both Christian and non-Christian—might be fashioned.

Notes

1. One wonders whether this perhaps a parenthetical remark indicating the response of someone departing after having been insulted.

2. This rubric introducing the song appears in Deuteronomy 31:30.

3. Given the references to divine names in the following lines, one wonders whether Hebrew *šādāy* might originally have read *šādāy*, "the Mountain One."

4. For a description of this word game, which involves the trading of insults about close relatives, see Clarence Major, *Juba to Jive: A Dictionary of African-American Slang* (New York: Penguin, 1994), 138, 149. A very basic definition of the concept, according to Major, includes "aimless talking; flirting; forceful talk; meaningless talk; to bluff; bullying; threatening to fight" (513; see 288 on this as synonymous with "loud talking").

5. Henry Louis Gates Jr., *The Signifying Monkey: A Theory of African-American Literary Criticism* (New York: Oxford University Press, 1988); Theodore O. Mason Jr., "Signifying," in *Africana: The Encyclopedia of the African and African-American Experience*, ed. J. Kwame Anthony Appiah and Henry Louis Gates Jr., 2nd ed. (New York: Oxford University Press, 2005); Zora Neale Hurston, *Mules and Men* (1935; repr., New York: HarperPerennial, 1990).

6. On signifying and the Yoruba God Esu, see Gates, *Signifying Monkey,* xix–xxviii, 21–22, 48–56.

7. Ibid., 52.

8. On this deity, see Olasope O. Oyelaran, "In What Tongue?" in *Orisa Devotion as World Religion: The Globalization of Yoruba Religious Culture*, ed. Jacob K. Olupona and Terry Rey (Madison: University of Wisconsin Press, 2008), 73–75; and Kathleen O'Connor, "Orishas," in Appiah and Gates, *Africana*, 295. On the image of the signifying monkey in African American discourse and its relationship to Esu, see Gates, *Signifying Monkey*, 52–54. Note in particular Gates's notion that he represents "the principle of self-consciousness in the black vernacular" (53).

"Somebody Done Hoodooed the Hoodoo Man"

Junior Wells, Balaam, and the Persistence of Conjure

NUMBERS 23:7-10

7.

So he *conjured*[1] the following *words of power*:[2]
Balak, the Moabite king,
Brought me from Aram;
From the eastern mountains
He implored:
"Come *cross* Jacob for me,
Come here and *fix* Israel!"[3]

―――

8-9.

For what reason should I *mess with* what El has not *crossed*?
Why should I *fix* what YHWH has not *fixed*?
I see them from mountain peaks,
Sense their presence from ancient hills.
They are Solitaries—Outsiders
Living on the move
And not aligned with
Other nations.

―――

10.

Who can count Jacob's dust?[4]
Or determine even a quarter of Israel?
May my soul die the death of those upright folk.

May my end be like theirs.

NUMBERS 23:18-24

18.
Once again Balaam *conjured words of power* and said:
Rise Balak and listen.
Pay attention to the Zipporite.

19.
El is neither a man that lies,
Nor a mortal that comforts himself.
Does he not follow through on what he says,
And stand by what he promises?

20.
Know this:
I came to bless, and did so.
What's more, it is irrevocable.

21.
I saw no iniquity in Jacob,
Noticed no trouble in Israel.
Their god, YHWH, is with them.
That Divine King placed his battle cry in their midst.

22.
El brought them from Egypt.
They are due great honor.
The *Great Bull's* horns are with them.

23.
There has been neither *fixing* in Jacob,
Nor *crossing* in Israel,
Since the time *El* issued a decree concerning these things.

24.
This people raises itself up like a lion,

Lifts itself up like a lion,
And does not rest until it eats prey
And consumes the blood of the slain.

———

NUMBERS 24:3-9
3.
So he *conjured* a third set of *powerful words* and said:

———

4.
Oracle of Balaam, the Beorite,
Saying of the man with deep insight,
Wisdom of the one who hears *El's* words,
Who sees *Shadday's* vision,
The one who falls down with opened eyes:

———

5.
How good are your tents, Jacob,
Your shelters, O Israel.

———

6.
As a property line they stretch out,
Like gardens by a river.
Yahweh planted them like aloe trees,
Like cedars near the waters.

———

7.
Let waters flow from their buckets.
May their seed flow forth like mighty waters.
May their king be exalted over Agag.
Let him carry away its dominion.

———

8.
El, the one leading them from Egypt,
Is like a bull's horns for them.
May they consume the nations, their adversaries.
Let them crush their bones.
May their arrows have shattering power.
9.

They crouch and stoop like a lion.
Like a lion, who will stand against them?
The one blessing them is indeed blessed.
The one cursing them is indeed cursed.

———

NUMBERS 24:15–24

15.

Therefore, he *conjured* this fourth set of *powerful words* and said:

Oracle of Balaam, the Beorite,
Saying of the man with deep insight.

———

16.

Wisdom of the one who hears *El's* words,
Who understands the knowledge of *Elyon—the Highest,*
Who sees Shadday's vision,
The one who falls down with opened eyes.

———

17.

I foresee something, but it is not immanent.
I discern an event, but it is not coming soon.
A star will come forth from Jacob,
A staff rises from Israel,
And shatters the territories of Moab.
Surely, it tears down the Shethites.

———

18.

Edom has become a possession,
A possession of its enemies is Seir.
Yet Israel is becoming mighty.

———

19.

Someone rules from Jacob;
He has destroyed the surviving cohort of the City.

———

20.

Then he conjured a fifth set of *powerful words*, against Amalek, and said:
Preeminent among nations was Amalek,
Yet its fate is destruction.

21.

He saw the Kenites and *conjured* this sixth *set of powerful words*:
Strong is your abode,
For your nest is in *the Rock* himself.

———

22.

For no Smith will light the forge,
When Asshur overtakes you.

———

23.

He then *conjured* a seventh, and final, set of *powerful words* and said:
Woe—Who can survive,
Once *El* sets this in motion?

———

24.

When ships come from Kittim,
When Asshur attacks,
When Eber mounts an assault
And He becomes a Destroyer?

Even in his seventies, Arnett Brown Sr. was a handsome mountain of a man: six feet, one inch tall, with a barrel chest, strong arms, weathered—yet incredibly soft—hands, a gentle demeanor, and a quick wit. One of ten children (six girls, four boys), he'd been raised in Carrollton, Virginia. He was a preacher's kid. His father had been a district elder in the African Methodist Episcopal (AME) Church. He'd been a farmer before moving to Baltimore, in the early 1900s. He was also a musician, a trumpet player. He came north, like many Black men from the South, to find employment. He worked at the steel mill in Sparrow's Point and then in the United States Postal Service. He played in nightclubs to supplement his income and rubbed shoulders with the likes of Eubie Blake. He fell in love with Virginia Cook, a green-eyed beauty who herself had come from Lancaster County, Virginia. She was a church-going woman. Before she agreed to marry him, she gave him an ultimatum: either the late-night music scene or her. He chose wisely.

They purchased a home together and raised two children, Elaine and Arnett Jr. They put both through college. They helped raise five grandchildren. He continued to make music: in the Sunday school of Payne Memorial AME Church, as a member of the Baltimore Post Office Band, and as director of the Baltimore Community Orchestra. He loved his family, his grandchildren in particular. The latter affectionately called him "Pop Pop." He worked hard and didn't suffer fools lightly. At home, he was a jack of all trades who could do everything from catching and scaling perch to making minor garment repairs on his foot-powered Singer sewing machine. His basement "den" was his sanctuary, workshop, and archive, the place where he saved sheet music, newspaper clippings, his children's old report cards and diplomas, and other family memorabilia. He was the de facto Brown family archivist, the griot. He kept his own counsel and believed strongly in the power of prayer. He was a teetotaler but had, for special occasions, a masonry jug of homemade dandelion wine in the cellar.

His faith was at once deep and pragmatic. He knew firsthand the challenges confronting people of color. He had little patience with unscrupulous people, especially if they occupied the pulpit. He took great pride in reasoning through biblical conundrums. One of his favorites had to do with whether the criminal crucified next to Jesus would be with him immediately in paradise (Luke 23:43). Another concerned the intellectual and rhetorical capacities of Balaam's donkey (Num. 22:23-33). The former was one of those imponderables that evangelical Christians of various stripes seem endlessly to mull and never resolve. The latter, the focus of an oft-heard gibe: the practice of labeling someone who'd done something unwise as "dumb as Balaam's ass." It was clear from his explanations of both that the Bible was, for him, the word of God. However, that did not stop him from engaging it, at times, in his own inimitably playful way. He was, for example, always quick to note, with a wry smile and a laugh, that Balaam's ass was an animal to be emulated. He called attention, in his own way, to the story's central paradox, in which a scene-stealing donkey makes a wizened seer look foolish.

Whatever one thinks of the age and provenance of the oracles embedded within the Balaam cycle and their relationship to the peripatetic holy man described therein, one's appreciation of both is enhanced when the text is read in light of the day-to-day life of people thought to possess the power to bless, curse, dream, and see what others cannot (Num. 22:6, 20-21, 31). From an Africana perspective, Numbers 22–24 paints a picture of the joys and challenges of being what in some parts of the Black world is called a "two-headed doctor" or practitioner of hoodoo. It specifically touches on the way such folks negotiate their relationships with clients; the particularities of their craft, that is, how they know what they know and accomplish what they set out to do; and the unpredictability associated with being a conduit of the numinous and ineffable. In the latter category, Balaam recognizes that he has been hired to use his power with words to cause harm to Israel. He also knows that he is subject to certain limitations (22:18) that are divine in origin. To flout them would be ill advised and dangerous. His patron, Balak, expects him, using the African American lexicon of conjure, to "fix," "cross," "trick," or "hoodoo" (curse) Israel.[5] Instead, he comes to realize that all bets are off when, to quote an old Junior Wells song, "somebody done hoodooed the Hoodoo Man."[6]

Based on all of the apparent biblical prohibitions against religious practices that fall outside of a fairly well-defined prophetic or priestly mainstream (such as Exod. 22:18, 34:13; Deut. 18:10-15; Judg. 2:2; Mal. 3:5; Rev. 21:8, 22:15), one might legitimately ask, What could the world of Africana conjure possibly have to say to that of the Bible? A close reading of the aforementioned texts, the Balaam tradition, and secondary literature on conjure reveals, not surprisingly, that ancient Near Eastern cosmologies have some elements in common with those West African worldviews that are the matrix out of which African American hoodoo grew.[7] For example, Jean-Jacques Glassner says the following of ancient Mesopotamia's semiotic universe:

> For the Mesopotamians, the universe was a dense and complex network of sympathies and antipathies that drew various objects and beings together or apart. Throughout the cosmos, beings and elements adjusted to one another and communicated between themselves.[8]

He goes on to say that humans, flora, fauna, and the world they inhabit are governed by the "essential principle of similitude according to which the similar has an effect on the similar."[9] To a great extent, these assertions apply in equal measure within ancient Egypt, Canaan, Israel, and Anatolia. The work of Robert Farris Thompson on Yoruba, Kongo, Mande, and Ejagham traditions and their adaptations in the Americas and the Caribbean makes clear that this is an Atlantic World cultural continuum in which the seen and unseen worlds are, as it were, woven into a single fabric. Thus, considerable light can be shed on stories like that of Balaam through a comparison of biblical traditions about him to, for example, the Yoruba concept of àshe, the nkisi lore of the Bakongo, the Mande notion of *woron*, and Ejagham *nsibidi* esotericism.[10] From such an Africana perspective, Balaam's exploits can be seen as those of a man possessing, and skilled in the channeling of, *àshe*, "the power-to-make-things-happen."[11] His oracular pronouncements amount to verbal, rather than physically inscribed, *nsibidi*—what Thompson designates as "signs embodying many powers, including the essence of all that is valiant, just, and ordered."[12] As Balak's retainer, Balaam was expected to be a *ndoki*, a "sorcerer" who exploited others' fears.[13] Instead, he comes to realize that he is no match for the *nkisi* Israel possesses: YHWH's incomparable "battle cry" (Num. 23:21).[14] The text suggests that when *Jah* is one's opponent, those possessing *woron*—literary and artistic adeptness[15]—know when to yield.

Although such an interpretation does not conform, in the strict sense, to a strategy that makes the Balaam from Deir Alla the primary conversation partner for understanding the background and significance of Numbers 23–24, it does offer a way of thinking about how Africana readers might succeed in following the lead of Theophus Smith and fashion what he terms a "conjurational spirituality" through an engagement with early Hebrew poetry.[16] It might even be possible to develop new forms of Christian popular piety and ministry that are inclusive in their embrace of indigenous cultural elements, particularly those from the larger Africana world. In order for this to happen, theologians will need to become more familiar with African and African-Diasporan religious traditions through reading and firsthand experience. For example, direct exposure to twenty-first-century urban conjure through conversations with practitioners and discovery-based learning may engender greater appreciation of this amalgam in which African, African American, Roman Catholic, Protestant Christian, kabbalistic, popular German, Western esoteric, Native American, and other elements have met and continue to converge. It is likely also to reveal the length and breadth of what has been a fruitful, largely unofficial, and publicly unacknowledged conversation between peoples of African descent, the Christian faith, and the Black church about how to construct an Africana religious ecology that honors the diversity of this ethos and promotes well-being and freedom. An examination of how Africana conjure's constitutive elements are related to the those actions and objects classed as "sacramentals" within Roman Catholicism (such as ritual performances; the sacralization of oil, water, salt, herbs, various foods, clothing, personal effects, and objects; candles; and the liturgical use of statuary)[17] may prove to be foundational in establishing parameters for modern spiritualities of resistance that place the means for mediating access to *àshe* in the hands of those most in need of direct access to it.

Such an interpretation is not likely to assuage the fears of many within the Christian mainstream that conjure—or any other manifestation of indigenous Africana spirituality—is aberrant and heterodox. The challenge for the future will be in helping critics appreciate that indigenous traditions are, at least in the Americas, Africana responses to an ethnocide begun in the Middle Passage. They offer an alternative to cosmologies in which Africa and its peoples are objects to be commodified. Such an effort inevitably will call attention to the fact that within the Africana ethos, all religious functionaries—whether preacher, priest, imam, rabbi, or rootworker—are expected to be capable of addressing the full range of life circumstances that confront women and men of African descent in day-to-day life. Moreover, in so doing, they need to heed the lessons taught by the biblical lore related to Balaam and his donkey.

Those capable of and committed to serving the needs of the global Africana community need a diverse repertoire of skills drawn, at least in part, from customs within that world that have been forced underground by the narrow-mindedness of well-meaning Christian evangelists and the pressure to leave behind those vestiges of the past that inhibit cultural assimilation. Thus, votive candles lit adjacent to a parish prie-dieu are likely to be deemed acceptable, whereas their red and green counterparts lit in a new home to evoke love and prosperity within it are not; and holy water sprinkled by a cleric to bless a crucifix in a parish is sure to be seen as a perfectly acceptable liturgical act, whereas the sprinkling of the same near a threshold to keep evil at bay may raise eyebrows. In the end, those providing pastoral care to people of color, particularly those of African descent for whom ancestral lore is their most cherished possession, would do well to familiarize themselves with these old traditions.

This is certain to be a difficult process to facilitate. Those most knowledgeable of this cultural milieu and its more esoteric practices are not usually found on the faculties of seminaries and divinity schools. The academy tends not to be the training ground for two-headed doctors. The guardians of this tradition pass it on in hushed whispers, via informal apprenticeships, and in spiritual-supply stores, where the measure of success is efficacy rather than tenure. For the rootworker and conjure to be brought from the theological and academic margin to the mainstream, and for an appreciation of conjure to be cultivated within the academy and the church, what the late Robert Hood refers to as the "cloak of invisibility over the theological integrity and thought of Afro cultures" has to be lifted within the core and ancillary disciplines of theology, in particular that branch devoted to the cure of souls.[18] Hood left open the issue of whether an "alliance" between traditional "Eurocentric"

Christian theology and "black cultures and thought" could be forged, a coalition that would effectively raise the aforementioned veil.[19] More than two decades after posing this question, Hood's query remains unanswered.

Nonetheless, there remains an air of hope for progress to be made. With confidence in large-scale religious institutions waning, indigenous Atlantic World traditions may prove to be of increasing interest to Africana and other seekers looking to create alternative ways of living and being—approaches that honor the particularities of the various African and Diasporan locales in which they "live, move, and exist" (Acts 17:28).

Notes

1. Throughout this book, I appeal to the lexicon of the African American amalgam of lore relating to healing and harming through the use of words, herbs, plants, and other power-infused objects known by names such as *hoodoo*, *rootwork*, and *conjure* to render those Hebrew terms that relate to comparable activities in early Israel. Used as a verb, *conjure* can refer to any of the aforementioned practices deployed for the benefit or to the detriment of oneself or others.

2. The meaning of the Hebrew word here rendered by the New Revised Standard Version (NRSV) as "oracle" has more the meaning of an utterance with spiritual efficacy.

3. "Crossing," "fixing," and "messing with" typically denote the negative or harmful dimensions of conjure.

4. One cannot help but be reminded of the tradition of graveyard dirt, or "Goofer dust," that is part of Africana pharmacopoeia. See Robert Farris Thompson, *Flash of the Spirit: African and Afro-American Art and Philosophy* (New York: Vintage, 1984), 105.

5. On the meaning of these terms, and others related to this body of African American traditions, see Jeffrey E. Anderson, *Hoodoo, Voodoo, and Conjure: A Handbook*, Greenwood Folklore Handbooks (Westport, CT: Greenwood, 2008), 2–3.

6. This is the refrain from track 7, "Hoodoo Man Blues," on the expanded rerelease of Junior Wells's classic 1965 album *Hoodoo Man Blues* (Delmark, 2011).

7. See, for example, Yvonne P. Chireau, *Black Magic: Religion and the African American Conjuring Tradition* (Berkeley: University of California Press, 2003); Jeffrey E. Anderson, *Conjure in African American Society* (Baton Rouge: Louisiana State University Press, 2005), and *Hoodoo, Voodoo, and Conjure*; and Stephanie Mitchem, *African American Folk Healing* (New York: New York University Press, 2007).

8. Jean-Jacques Glassner, "The Use of Knowledge in Ancient Mesopotamia," in *Civilizations of the Ancient Near East*, ed. Jack M. Sasson (Peabody, MA: Hendrickson, 2000), 1817–18.

9. Ibid., 1818.

10. Thompson, *Flash of the Spirit,* 5–7, 105–7, 117–45, 196.

11. Ibid., 5.

12. Ibid., 227.

13. Ibid., 107.

14. Thompson defines the *nkisi* as "a strategic object in black Atlantic art, said to effect healing and other phenomena" (ibid., 117).

15. Ibid., 196.

16. Theophus Smith, *Conjuring Culture: Biblical Formations of Black America* (New York: Oxford University Press, 1994), viii.

17. This is a representative sample of practices enumerated by Ann Ball in her popular treatment of the subject, *The How-To Book of Sacramentals: Everything You Need to Know but No One Ever Taught You* (Huntington, IN: Our Sunday Visitor, 2005).

18. Robert Hood, *Must God Remain Greek? Afro Cultures and God-Talk* (Minneapolis: Fortress Press, 1990), 252.

19. Ibid., 253.

8

"Something Got a Hold of Me"
1 Samuel 2 and Aged Black Bodies

1 SAMUEL 2

1.

Then Hannah prayed:
My heart rejoices in YHWH.
My strength is bolstered by *Jah*.
My mouth speaks out against my enemies,
Because I celebrate your saving power!

2.

There is no Holy One like YHWH.
In fact, there is none except you!
There is no *Rock* like our god.

3.

Don't be excessively haughty in speech.
Do not permit arrogance to proceed from your lips.
Jah's knowledge is vast.
Does he not assess (our) deeds?

4.

Warriors' bows are shattered,
Yet, the ordinary become mighty.

5.

The wealthy hire themselves out for food,
But the hungry are sated.

The barren woman bears seven children,
While she who has many sons suffers.

6.

YHWH causes death and life.
He brings one down and raises one up from Sheol.

7.

Jah creates poverty and wealth.
He bestows shame and honor.

8.

He raises the poor from the dust,
Elevates the needy from the ash heaps
To sit with nobility;
Indeed, he gives them a glorious throne as an inheritance,
Because to YHWH belong Earth's pillars.
He is the one who set the world upon them.

9.

He watches the sojourn of his faithful ones,
Though the evil stumble about in darkness,
For a person does not prevail by mere force.

10.

Jah shatters his opponents.
He thunders against them in the heavens.
He judges Earth's full extent,
Strengthens his king,
And greatly empowers his anointed.

It was supposed to be nothing more than a group-bonding event. Black fraternities do this kind of thing all the time. It was a way of building rapport and doing something good for the community. However, Christmas caroling on that cold late-December day became something far more remarkable. I should have known what I was in for when we gathered to organize our carpool trek to several South Bend nursing homes and began with a moment of prayer. It became all too clear when, having arrived at the first of many convalescent centers and having sung several Yuletide standards, one of the women in our ensemble started an impromptu gospel song by intoning "Jesus" and another member of our group started to "testify." "We're not just here to sing," he said. "We're here expecting someone's affliction to be healed." I knew then that we were "having church" and were on a "mission."

Later that afternoon, when we ended our final visitation with everyone in our group "moaning" the old James Cleveland tune "Something Got a Hold of Me," I sensed deep down that I'd been part of something special. We'd given a little bit of hope to many a forgotten soul. We'd made Hannah's God present in some places where hope had literally "gone to die," and helped heal Black bodies that had been forgotten, broken, and cast aside. We'd participated in the eschatological inversion of the status quo in the here and now, if only for a moment or two. Our songs were prayers of deliverance, a clear signal that the one "who brings one down and raises one up" (1 Sam. 2:6) sees, knows of, and cares about the afflictions of those who suffer—especially the African American Hannahs into whose faces I gazed on that day.

Looking back on that excursion and thinking about Hannah's prayer in 1 Samuel 2 bring back haunting memories of the outspoken and audacious Black women whose timely, often prayerful interventions saved my life, whose practical fusion of common sense and Christian spirituality enabled them to pray with passion, work their fingers raw, and plan strategically for the care of themselves and their families. I know of one who worked as a domestic for a wealthy family. They gave her cash to have their laundry professionally done. She took the laundry to her own home, hand-washed it, and squirreled away the money to buy her great-grandchildren savings bonds—an act of everyday resistance, a means of "making a way from no way."

Stories abound of Black women who have relied on mother wit and common sense derived from years of struggle to navigate an at-times-overtly-hostile American landscape. They passed on timeless truths to those given into their charge, one of which is a pivotal theme in 2 Samuel 22. It is that reversals, of all kinds, are to be expected within the Africana world. Some of them, in fact, conform in a relatively straightforward way to the pattern found in the song of Hannah, in which "the wealthy hire themselves out for food, but the hungry are sated" (1 Sam. 2:6). The abolition of the transatlantic slave trade, the Emancipation Proclamation, the election (and subsequent reelection) of the first African American president in the United States—such are instances when "business as usual" in the political sphere has been interrupted and an inversion in the expected order of things has taken place. In such instances, the appropriateness of the advice given in the statement: "a person does not prevail by mere force" (1 Sam. 2:9), or in Paul's assertion that "power is brought to its ideal expression in weakness" (2 Cor. 12.9) is confirmed. However, there are other cases in which social, political, and economic turnarounds leave those already on the bottom of the hierarchy of power and prestige, through strange twists of fate, even further disenfranchised. Such asymmetrical reversals are not uncommon in African American life. Leaders die tragically. The stories of everyday heroes are lost. The innocent lose their lives in senseless acts of violence. Our venerable elders, many of whom lack sufficient resources to ensure comfort in their golden years, end their lives forgotten and alone. (Perhaps this is one reason why the lore of trickster deities persists in our collective imaginary.) Such asymmetrical reversals must clearly have been part of the life experience of women in ancient Israel. In spite of the cultural realities to which narratives and poems about Deborah, Jael, Hannah, and other biblical women point, the social milieu of the ancient Near East was not one that afforded women full equality with men or independent agency. The same is true, unfortunately, for much of the Africana world.

Thus, an Africana reading of Hannah's story and prayer must take seriously one remarkable paradox: if the most poignant sign of hope that can be given to a woman incapable of bearing children is that she will be able to conceive, give birth, and receive renown through a male child born to her, then one of the "opponents" that even YHWH appears incapable of "shattering" (1 Sam. 2:10) is patriarchy itself.

Harmolodic Blues and an Esoteric Mash-Up

Reengaging 2 Samuel 1; 22 (Psalm 18); 23; and Three Ancient Psalms (68, 72, and 78)

2 SAMUEL 1:18-27

17–18.

David *sang the blues* concerning Saul and his son Jonathan. Furthermore, he instructed that the Judahites learn the *bow blues*. It is written as follows in the Book of Jashar:

19.

The glory of Israel is upon your high places—slain. How is it that mighty warriors have fallen?

20.

Report it not in Gath, Do not spread good tidings in the streets of Ashkelon; Lest Philistine women rejoice And foreign women exult.

21.

The mountains in Gilboa Have neither dew nor rain upon them; Neither do the fields produce any yield, Because the shield of warriors was defiled there, The shield of Saul, devoid of its anointing.

22.

Jonathan's bow did not shun The blood of the slain, the flesh of mighty men, Nor did the sword of Saul return empty.

23.
Saul and Jonathan,
Beloved and lovely in life and death;
They were not divided.
The two were swifter than eagles,
Mightier than lions.
24.
Women of Israel—weep for Saul,
The one who clothed you in scarlet, with luxuries,
The one heaping up ornaments of gold upon your raiment.
25.
How is it that mighty warriors have fallen
In the midst of battle?
Why does Jonathan lay slain upon your high places?
26.
Jonathan, my brother, I am greatly distressed.
You were exceedingly dear to me.
More extraordinary was your love to me
Than that of women.
27.
How is it that mighty warriors have fallen,
The implements of war destroyed?

2 SAMUEL 22

1.
David gave voice to his *blues* in this Divine song,
When YHWH rescued him from the power of all his enemies,
And from the hand of Saul.
What follows is the rendition:

———

2-3.
YHWH is my Rock and Stronghold,
The God of my Rock in whom I trust,
My Shield and the Horn of my Salvation,
My stronghold, refuge, and savior.
You saved me from violence.

———

4.

I call to *Jah*—the praiseworthy One
And he will rescue me from my enemies.

———

5.

Because the breakers of Death surround me,
The chords of Belial overwhelm me.

———

6.

The chords of Sheol surround me,
Before me are the snares of Mot.

———

7.

In my distress I called to YHWH,
To *El*, my God;
I called, and he heard my voice in his Sacred Place.
My plea reached his ears.

———

8.

Earth's foundations rocked,
The heavens rolled.
Everything shook back and forth,
Because of his anger.

———

9.

Smoke went up from his nose,
All-consuming flames from his mouth.
Charcoal burned within it.

———

10.

He stretched out the heavens and came down.
A dark cloud was beneath his feet.

———

11.

He rode a Cherub and flew.
He was seen on the Wind's wings.

———

12.

He surrounded himself with darkness,

raging storms, and dense clouds.

———
13.
From his Shining Presence
Fiery coals burn.

———
14.
YHWH thunders from heaven,
Elyon—the Highest—lets loose his voice.

———
15.
He dispatched arrows and dispersed them.
Lightning he sent to confuse them.

———
16.
The watercourses of the Sea were revealed,
The foundations of the earth were uncovered
At the rebuke of YHWH,
From the wind issuing from his nose.

———
17.
He sent from his lofty place and rescued me,
He caused me to be lifted from the midst of mighty waters.

———
18.
He rescued me from my powerful enemies,
The mighty who hate me.
Indeed, they were stronger than me.

———
19.
They confronted me on the day of my crisis;
Jah served as my supporter.

———
20.
He brought me to a broad place.
He rescued me because he favored me.

———
21.
YHWH dealt favorably with me because of my righteousness.

Because my hands were clean, he brought me back.

———

22.

Because I stayed on YHWH's paths,
And did no wicked thing before my God.

———

23.

Because all of his commands were before me,
Given that I did not turn away from his statutes,

———

24.

And am blameless before him—
Keeping myself assiduously from doing evil—

———

25.

Jah brought me back because of my innocence,
Because I was blameless in his eyes.

———

26.

With the righteous, you are faithful.
With the warrior, blameless.

———

27.

With the pure, you are pure.
With the dishonest, you are deceptive.

———

28.

You save the poor
But scrutinize the high and mighty to bring them down.

———

29.

You are my light, O YHWH,
Yes, *Jah* sheds light on my *dark existence*.[1]

———

30.

Because of you I can run with warriors;
With you, O my god, I can surmount a wall.

———

31.

As for this god—his way is perfect;
The word of YHWH has been tested.
He is a shield for all who take refuge in him.

—
32.

Who is a real deity, save *Jah?*
Who is a Rock other than our god?

—
33.

This *El* is my strength—a Mighty Warrior;
He makes my journey steady and sure.

—
34.

He makes my feet like those of a doe,
He establishes a foothold for me in inaccessible places.

—
35.

He prepares me to do battle
And prepares my arms to bend the bronze bow.

—
36.

You give me your saving shield,
And your gentleness has strengthened.

—
37.

You prepare for me a wide path
So that my feet do not slip.

—
38.

Let me pursue and destroy my enemies.
Let me not return until they are brought to an end.

—
39.

Allow me to annihilate and crush them,
So that they are unable to stand
And fall beneath my feet.

—
40.

You empower me with strength for war.

You humble those who stand against me.

———
41.
You hand over my enemies to me,
The necks of those that hate me,
So I can destroy them.

———
42.
They look around, but there is no Savior.
They turn to YHWH,
But he does not answer them.

———
43.
Let me beat them down like earthen dust,
As mud in the streets let me pound and pulverize them.

———
44.
You rescued me from the contentious actions of my people.
You watched over me as a leader of nations.
People that do not know me serve me.

———
45.
Foreigners cower in my presence,
They acknowledge and heed me.

———
46.
Foreign peoples are disheartened,
Though they gird themselves within their fortresses.

———
47.
Jah lives! Blessed is my Rock.
Let the *Divine Rock—my Salvation—*be exalted.

———
48.
This god is *my Avenger,*
The *One Who Humiliates People before Me,*

———
49.
The *One Rescuing Me from Enemies:*

You elevate me above those who oppose me.
You deliver me from violent men.

———

50.
Therefore, I praise you, O YHWH, among the peoples;
I will sing of your Name.

———

51.
A *Saving Tower* for his king,
One Who Is Faithful to his anointed,
For David and his progeny eternally.

———

2 Samuel 23

1.
These are the last words of David:
Oracle of David—son of Jesse,
Powerful words of the warrior,
The one established on high,
Anointed One of Jacob's God,
Hero of Israel's songs.

———

2.
The spirit of YHWH speaks through me,
His word is on my tongue.

———

3.
The *God of Israel* called,
Israel's Rock instructed me as follows:

———

"The *Righteous Ruler of Humanity*,
The *One Governing by Divine Fear*.

———

4.
"Is akin to the light of Dawn,
The solar light that shines forth,
A morning without clouds.
From such brightness, from the Dew itself,

Sprouts grass from the Earth."

—

5.

For this reason,
My house belongs to El.
Because an eternal covenant he set before me—
Established with everyone and preserved,
For my complete salvation and delight;
Does he not cause things to grow?

—

6.

Yet Wickedness has spread like thorns.
Its totality cannot be grasped in hand.

—

7.

For when one touches it,
One feels the sting of iron and wooden spears,
And it burns intensely like fire inside.

PSALM 68

—

1.

To the overseer, a *mash-up*,[2]
A song belonging to David:

—

2.

Let God get up.
Let his enemies run away.
Let those who despise him
Flee his presence.

—

3.

As smoke dissipates,
May you disperse them.
As wax melts before fire,
Let the wicked perish
From God's presence.

—

4.

As for the righteous,
Let them rejoice.
Let them celebrate
Exuberantly before God.

———
5.

Sing to God.
Praise his name.
Shout out to the Cloud Rider
Whose name is *Jah.*
Rejoice before him!

———
6.

Father of orphans,
Judge of widows:
God is in his holy place.

———
7.

God finds homes for the abandoned.[3]
He leads prisoners
To safe, lush surroundings.
But the rebellious must remain
In arid wastelands.

———
8.

O God, when you went out to lead your people,
When you marched into Jeshimon—Selah,

———
9.

Ancient Earth reeled,
The Heavens shed tears,
In the presence of *Elohim,*
The *One from Sinai,*
Before *Elohim—Israel's God.*

———
10.

You granted abundant rain, O God.
When your inheritance languished,
You built them up.

———
11.

Your flock established a home within her;[4]
You assisted the poor, O *Elohim*.

———
12.

The Lord provides inspiration[5]
For those bearing glad tidings to the masses.

———
13.

Kings of armies run to and fro.
The queen[6] divides spoil at home.

———
14.

Indeed, the former dwell within sheepfolds.
Like the wings of a dove,
The latter is adorned with silver,
And her accoutrements are of gleaming gold.

———
15.

When *Shadday* routed the kings,
It snowed in Zalmon.

———
16.

O Holy Mountain,
Mount Bashan,
O Powerful Mountain,
Mount Bashan,

———
17.

Why are you so jealous, Majestic Heights,
Of the mount God desires to declare home?
Jah will reign there eternally.

———
18.

God's chariots number twenty thousand,
Indeed thousands of thousands.
The Lord, whose sanctuary is Sinai,
Rides with them.

—
19.
You ascended the heights.
You captured prisoners.
You received gifts from humankind.
Nonetheless, O rebellious ones,[7]
Jah reigns as god.

—
20.
Blessed is the Lord:
El, the one who supports us daily,
Is our salvation—Sela.
21.
El is for us a god who saves,
Indeed, *Jah* is a Lord
Who rescues us from Death.

—
22.
Elohim strikes the head of his enemies,
The skull and hair of
People strutting about in their guilt.

—
23.
The Lord has said:
"I will return from Bashan,
From the sea's depths,

—
24.
"So that you may take revenge—
Your feet covered in blood;
The tongues of your dogs as well;
Property from enemies—seized."[8]

—
25.
They gaze upon your festal liturgies, O *Elohim*,
Processions, O My God and King, in the Holy Place.

—
26.
Singers—go in front!

After them, the *strings*!
Tambourines—among the *Falsettos*!

27.

Within the congregations, bless *Elohim*.
Bless *Jah* from Israel's springs.

28.

There is Benjamin the Small One,
Leader of Judah's princely throng,
The nobility of Zebulun and Naphtali.

29.

Your god—your *Mighty One*—commands.
Assume control, O *Elohim*, in all that you do for us!

30.

From Jerusalem's temple,
Kings bring you gifts.

31.

Rebuke, O beasts, the reeds.
Do likewise, O congregation of nobles,
To those gathering the peoples:
Those trampling silver tribute,
Scattering the masses.
They are warmongers.

32.

Ambassadors come from Egypt.
Cush quickly embraces *Elohim*.

33.

Terrestrial Kingdoms, sing to *Elohim*!
Give praise to the Lord—Selah.

34.

Praise the *Celestial Rider*
Of Ancient Skies.

Know this:
He speaks with a most powerful voice.

―――

35.
Acknowledge *Elohim's* strength:
The one who rules Israel.
His majesty and power
Are manifest in the Heavens.

―――

36.
An awe-inspiring Divine wonder
Are your sanctuaries, O *El*.
O Israel, He is the Source of Everyone's
Power and Strength.
Bless God!

―――

PSALM 72

1.
Concerning Solomon:
Grant, O God, your justice to the King,
Your righteousness to his son.

―――

2.
May he judge your people with righteousness,
Your afflicted with justice.

―――

3.
May the mountains bring peace to the people,
And the hills righteousness.

―――

4.
May he provide justice for the poor masses,
Salvation for the children of the destitute.
Let him crush oppressors.

―――

5.
May they fear you with the Sun.

And the moon for all generations.

———

6.
May he rain down
Like dew upon that which has been mown,
Like showers dripping on the Earth.

———

7.
May the righteous flourish in his lifetime,
And peace until the moon is no more.
8.
May he rule from sea to sea,
From the great river to Earth's full expanse.

———

9.
Let the desert inhabitants bow in his presence,
And his enemies lick dust.

———

10.
As for the kings of Tarshish and the Coastlands,
Let them pay tribute.
Let the rulers of Sheba and Saba draw near with gifts.

———

11.
Let all kings worship him,
And every nation serve him,

———

12.
Because he delivers the poor,
The one crying out for help,
The destitute,
And the one lacking assistance.

———

13.
He has compassion
On the humiliated and penniless,
And rescues the lives of the impoverished.

———

14.

He redeems their lives
From oppression and violence,
And their blood is precious to him.

———
15.
May he thrive.
May people bring to him
Gold from Sheba.
Let them pray continually for him,
And bless him daily.

———
16.
May there be abundant grain
In the land and on the mountaintops.
May its sprouts sway in the breeze
The way Lebanon quakes.
May cities blossom,
Like grassy fields.

———
17.
May his name be eternal.
May it endure like the Sun.
May all bless themselves through him,
And let every nation declare him just.

———
18.
Blessed is *Jah*:
Elohim—God of Israel,
The Unparalleled Wonder Worker;

———
19.
And eternally blessed
Be his Glorious Name.
May Earth's great expanse
Be filled with his glory,
Amen, indeed.

———
20.
This ends the prayers of David,

Jesse's child.

——

PSALM 78

1.

An *esoteric poem*[9] of Asaph:
Listen, my people, to my tale,
Heed the words of my mouth.

——

2.

Allow me to give voice to a parable,
To speak of ancient riddles:

——

3.

Things we ourselves heard and learned
That our ancestors recounted to us.

——

4.

We will not conceal these things from their children.
To the generation following us
We will recount *Jah's* praises:
The powerful acts and wondrous deeds he accomplished.

——

5.

He established testimony in Jacob.
Torah he placed in Israel,
Which he commanded our ancestors
To teach to their children,

——

6.

So the next generation knows.
Children they will bear
Will grow up and tell their children.

——

7.

They will place their trust in *Elohim*.
They will neither forget *El's* deeds
Nor forsake the things he commands.

8.

They will not be akin to their parents:
A generation both stubborn and rebellious,
With unsteady hearts
And spirits unable to trust *El*.

9.

Children of Ephraim:
Armed with Archers,
They cowered on the day of battle.

10.

They did not keep *Elohim's* covenant,
And refused to behave according to his laws.

11.

They forgot the deeds and wonders
He showed them.

12.

With their ancestors looking on,
He *conjured* wondrous things:
In the Egypt land,
The fields of Zoan.

13.

He cleaved the sea,
And led them across.
The waters therein
Stood still like a wall.

14.

Daily, he led them by a cloud,
By a flaming light each night.

15.

He broke open rocks in the desert,
And allowed them to drink abundantly

16.
From the primordial depths.
Streams issued from stones;
He made rivers of water flow.

17.
Yet they sinned again and again,
Continually rebelled in the desert
Against *Elyon—the Highest.*

18.
They tested *El* in their hearts,
Asking to receive food for their souls.

19.
They *signified* on *Elohim*
And said:
"Can *El* set a table in the Wilderness?

20.
"Sure—he struck a rock
And water flowed;
Streams did come forth.
But can he provide bread
Or muster up some meat for his people?"

21.
Consequently, *Jah* heard these things
And was angry;
Divine Fire was ignited against Jacob,
Celestial Wrath kindled against Israel,

22.
Because they lacked faith in *Elohim,*
Didn't trust in his saving power.

23.
So he issued a command to the clouds above,

Opened the celestial doors,

24.

And *manna* for them to eat rained down.
He gave them heavenly grain.

25.

Humans ate the bread of immortals.
He sent them abundant provisions.

26.

He led them east by Heavenly signs,
And southward by his power,

27.

And showered them with meat
As plentiful as dust,
Winged birds as numerous
As the sea's sands.

28.

They fell in the midst of their encampment,
All around their tents,

29.

And they ate and were exceedingly satisfied;
He gave them what they wanted.

30.

Their desire not yet a distant memory,
Food yet to be consumed and digested,

31.

Divine Anger flared against them,
And he killed many from among the privileged
And cut down Israel's young and powerful.

32.

In spite of all this,

They sinned again
And were unmoved by his powerful *conjurings*.

———

33.
So they spent their days in emptiness,
And their years in abject terror.

———

34.
So, he killed them.
Then, they inquired after him,
Indeed, returned to and sought *El.*

———

35.
They recalled that *Elohim* was their *Rock*,
That *El Elyon—the Peerless God—*was their *Redeemer*.

———

36.
Yet they were simplistic in their affirmations,
And deceptive in their contemplation of him.

———

37.
Their hearts were not firmly set on him.
They didn't trust in his covenant.

———

38.
Nonetheless, He was Compassionate.
He forgave their sin
And did not destroy them.
He greatly restrained his anger
And did not unleash all of his rage.

———

39.
He remembered that they were mortal:
A wind that blows once—never to return.

———

40.
How often they did challenge his authority in the desert,
And grieve him in Jeshimon.

———

41.

They would continually test *El*,
Provoke *Israel's Holy One*.

___

42.

They would forget his incomparable *Hand*,
The day when he saved them from dire straits,

___

43.

When he *conjured* signs in Egypt,
Wonders in Zoan's wasteland.

___

44.

He transformed their Nile tributaries to blood,
And they were not able to drink from their streams.

___

45.

He infested them with swarms of flies
That consumed them,
And frogs that laid them waste.

___

46.

He gave grasshoppers their produce,
The fruit of their labor to locust swarms.

___

47.

He destroyed their vineyards with hail,
Their sycamores with frost.

___

48.

He consigned their livestock to hail,
Their cattle to pestilence.

___

49.

Against them he unleashed his burning anger,
Wrath, Indignation, and Distress:
A deputation of devastating spiritual messengers.

___

50.

He carefully considered the course of his anger,
And did not spare them from death.
He delivered them up to Plague.

51.

He struck down all of Egypt's firstborn,
The most gifted in their households.

52.

He led his own people from there like sheep,
And guided them as a flock through the wilderness.

53.

He guided them to a safe place,
So they were no longer fearful;
The sea itself covered their adversaries.

54.

He brought them to his holy precinct,
This very mountain,
Acquired by his *Right Hand*.

55.

He dispossessed the nations for them,
Established their inheritance,
And enabled the Tribes of Israel
To live in their tents.

56.

Yet, again, they tested,
And rebelled against *Elohim—the Highest*.
They refused to honor his testimonies.

57.

They turned their backs,
And behaved treacherously like their forebears.
They failed like an unreliable bow.

58.

They angered him with their high places,
Made him jealous with their idols.

———

59.

Elohim heard, burned with anger,
And rejected Israel totally.

———

60.

He left his Shiloh shrine,
The tent where he dwells with humanity.

———

61.

He handed over their power to captivity,
Their glory to the authority of foes.

———

62.

He consigned his people to the sword,
And raged against his inheritance.

———

63.

Fire devoured their young men,
Their young women did not sing praises.

———

64.

Their priests fell by the sword,
And their widows did not weep.

———

65.

But the Lord awakened from sleep,
Like a warrior overcoming a hangover.

———

66.

He struck the backs of his enemies,
And showed them unending reproach.

———

67.

He rejected Joseph's tents,
Did not designate the tribe of Ephraim.

———

68.

Instead, he chose the tribe of Judah,
And Mount Zion, which he adores.

———

69.

He built—as a place of exaltation—his sanctuary;
Like Earth itself, its foundation is eternal.

———

70.

He chose David as his servant,
Took him from the sheepfolds,

———

71.

From watching over young animals,
He brought him
To be a shepherd for Jacob, his people,
For Israel, his kin.

———

72.

May he lead them with integrity of heart,
And guide them with deft hands.

———

Collections abound in the First and Second Testaments. Both are carefully crafted miscellanies. The sources brought together are sometimes explicitly named, such as the book of YHWH's wars (Num. 21:14), the book of Jashar (2 Sam. 1:18), the book of Solomon's words (1 Kgs. 11:41), the record of Judah's kings (1 Kgs. 14:29), and the record of Israel's kings (1 Kgs. 15:31). Some are set off by superscriptions, such as those psalms belonging to the Asaphite (50, 73–83) and the Korahite portions of the Psalter (42, 44–49, 84–85, 87–88). Still others are easily identifiable by internal genre markers, such as oracles (including Proverbs 30–31; Isaiah 13, 15; Nahum 1; and Habakkuk 1), personal letters (such as those of purported Pauline origin in the New Testament: 1 Thessalonians, 1 and 2 Corinthians, Romans, Galatians, Philippians, and Philemon),[10] parables (such as Matt. 13:3-9, 24-30, 44-50, and elsewhere), and signs (including John 2:1-11, 4:46-54, and 6:1-15). The factors contributing to the formation of such compilations vary. The same can be said of the ways they are used. Elsewhere, I argue that early Hebrew poetry, in its entirety, is a "virtual assemblage" whose purpose is to promote reflection on a host of vexing issues ranging from the opacity of the divine will to the insanity of war.[11] That larger corpus can be subdivided in any number of ways, based either on criteria derived internally or on interpretive models externally created and applied. One possibility involves treating 2 Samuel 1, 22 (Psalm 18), 23; and Psalms 68, 72, and 78 as an esoteric "mash-up" whose structure and literary cadences are reminiscent of harmolodic blues. The term *mash-up* is used in modern parlance with reference to a tangible product—musical, visual, digital, literary, ideational—that combines disparate and, in some cases, unlikely elements.[12] Harmolodic blues is a subgenre of music pioneered by James "Blood" Ulmer and Vernon Reid that applies the harmolodic jazz theory of Ornette Coleman to classical blues.[13] Of harmolodics, Coleman himself says:

—I play pure emotion

—In music, the only thaing [*sic*] that matters is whether you feel it or not

—Chords are just the name for sounds, which really need no names at all, as names are sometimes confusing

—Blow what you feel—anything. Play the thought, the idea in your mind—Break away from the convention and stagnation—escape![14]

A HARMOLODIC INTERLUDE

The temperature was in the single digits as he started the car and turned on the radio. It was an all-too-typical winter night in Montpelier, Vermont: clear, moonlit, impossibly frigid. On the way to a local carry-out joint, he heard a gravelly voice accompanied on guitar by a cacophony of strangely timed "free-form" minor chords.

> I'm gonna take my music back to the church,
> Where the blues was misunderstood.
> Some people think that it was songs of the devil,
> But it was the soul of a man for sure.

This wasn't the evocative half-speaking, half-singing of Sonny Boy Williamson. Neither was it the stirring warble of Johnny Drummer. This sound defied categorization. He heard the singer talk about wanting to become a "preacher" that could construct his own "church" based on the "concept of the Blues."

All were odd echoes in his mind of James Cone's classic theological reading of spirituals and blues.[15] But what could anyone make of this strange tune: no 1, 4, 5 chord progression, no A, B, C rhyming pattern? There was nothing here but an outpouring of emotion and James Blood Ulmer's vision of a blues lacking conventional structure, a free-form blues "idea" that could be used to investigate the transcendent.[16] Could an irregular and discordant expression of a genre already maligned and misunderstood within the Black church restore its soul, make it once again a crucible for the development of Africana spiritualities of resistance? Are symmetry, regularity, repetition, and structure inhibitors of freedom? Is an implicit harmolodic poetics the stimulus for the deformation of structures of oppression and the development of lifeways oriented toward unfettered individual expression? Is Psalm 68 the one composition in early Hebrew poetry that enshrines a notion somewhat akin to this in ancient Israel? Is it the center of gravity for the entire assemblage of Israel's earliest verse? Blues and Bible—who'll be ready to entertain that complementary juxtaposition? Strange things to begin pondering on a late-night food run. As he drove by the closed red doors of Christ Church, he couldn't help but ask himself, Will any of this "preach" for Anglicans? He still wonders.

———

Of what advantage is it to think of 2 Samuel 1, 22, 23; and Psalms 68, 72, and 78 as an esoteric harmolodic mash-up? Second Samuel 1:18-27 is a lament over the deaths of Saul and Jonathan at once haunting in its sorrowful reminiscence of two fallen warriors and biting in its critique of the strife that lays low those consumed by the desire for combat. Second Samuel 22:1-51 is a celebratory song set within a Deuteronomistic narrative of Davidic exploits whose strong mythic overtones call to mind the cosmic scope of YHWH's dominion, salvific reach, and empowering capabilities in the human realm.[17] Second Samuel 23:1-7 is a cryptic utterance attributed to David that uses evocative mythopoeic language to link just monarchic rule to divine governance and natural fecundity while at the same time highlighting the persistence of opposing forces both earthly and cosmic. Psalm 72 is an invocation for the prosperity of a royal heir that draws on at least one well-known ancient Near Eastern trope: royal responsibility for the care of marginal, poor, and dispossessed persons (vv. 12-14). Psalm 78, another enigmatic piece, rehearses the "ancient riddles" (v. 2) embedded into Israel's sacred epic. That story narrates a journey beginning with the handing down of Torah to the community (v. 5) and reaching its climax in the establishment of the Davidic monarchy (vv. 70-72).

Perhaps a solution is found in Psalm 68, an odd composition whose rhythms are uneven and whose themes range far and wide. Its strophes have the appearance of snapshots brought together to form a collage or strip quilt whose deeper meaning can be intuited only by pondering them both singly and as part of its atypical architecture.[18] One need not see the psalm as a catalog of opening lines from a selection of ancient poems now lost.[19] More accurate, perhaps, is Mitchell Dahood's conception of it as a hymn with three foci—the Egyptian defeat (vv. 2-7), the Israelite wilderness sojourn (vv. 2-9), and the occupation of Canaan (vv. 10-15)—whose latter portion "plays variations on these principal themes."[20] This apparent allusion to the world of music is consistent with an approach to Psalm 68 that views it as the paradigm and harmolodic core both for a mash-up of early Hebrew poems consisting of 2 Samuel 1, 22, 23; and Psalms 68, 72, and 78 and for the early Hebrew poetic corpus overall. As such, its tenuous balance between structure and antistructure is emblematic of the highs and lows of the journey described in Psalm 78. It is representative of the intractable problems of ensuring just governance, national prosperity, and the equitable treatment of the disenfranchised with which every ruler must wrestle (2 Sam. 23:1-7; Psalm 72). It symbolizes the unending cosmic struggle between the forces of life and death (2 Sam. 22:1-51). It is an iconic emblem of the irregularities, the unavoidably untidy aspects, of human life that those with unbridled power try, at times, to resolve through armed conflict (2 Sam. 1:19-27). As a whole, this small collection reminds readers that the rough terrain that Africana peoples often tread, the uncertainties with which they inevitably deal, and the unexpected twists and turns that their pilgrimage to freedom often takes are the great secret hidden in plain sight. It is within such anomalies that transcendence and human connectedness are mysteriously found in "blue notes" and songs whose jarring rhythms and peculiar melodies prohibit complacent listening and mindless consumption.

Notes

1. Here, one is reminded of the "dark script" metaphor used by Vincent Wimbush in "Interpreters: Enslaving/Enslaved/Runagate," *Journal of Biblical Literature* 130, no. 1 (2011): 5–24, to describe the exigencies of Africana life.

2. Whatever the designation *mizmôr* may have originally meant, here it may connote a disparate conflation of ideas, themes, and random thoughts—a "mash-up," as it were, of completely disparate elements that embodies the mixing of discourses typifying life in diaspora.

3. In Hebrew, the word used connotes those who are alone and solitary. This suggests, to me, abandonment by those who would provide a protective social network.

4. The antecedent to which this word refers is Ancient Earth, conceived of both as female deity and as terrestrial abode of humanity.

5. A more literal translation of the Hebrew here is "the Lord gives a word." The sense appears to be that God is the source of words delivered by those sharing "glad tidings."

6. The literal meaning here is "the beautiful one of the house," a generic reference perhaps to the one whose role is juxtaposed to that of a monarch within a royal domicile.

7. The Hebrew syntax here is unclear. I treat the conjunction and particle *wǝ - 'ap* as a disjunctive element introducing a vocative.

8. The syntax of these lines is difficult. The passage appears to be a free-associative musing that calls to mind fragmentary scenes from battle, bloodshed, and booty claimed from defeated adversaries.

9. Given the use of the words *māšāl* (parable) and *ḥîdôt minnî - qedem* (ancient riddles), this translation of Hebrew *maśkîl* is more than reasonable.

10. This list, considered common knowledge among many Bible scholars, is taken from Harold W. Attridge et al., eds., *The Harper Collins Study Bible*, rev. ed. (New York: HarperOne, 2006), 1908.

11. Hugh R. Page Jr., "Myth and Social Realia in Ancient Israel: Early Hebrew Poems as Folkloric Assemblage," in *Myth and Scripture: Contemporary Perspectives on Religion, Language, and Imagination*, ed. J. Dexter E. Callender (Atlanta, GA: Society of Biblical Literature, forthcoming).

12. Here I adhere to, and expand upon, the basic definition of *mash-up* offered by the online version of the *Merriam-Webster Dictionary*, m-w.com, http://www.merriam-webster.com/dictionary/mash-up. There is, as one might expect, no entry for the word in the *Oxford English Dictionary*. In urban and Internet cultures, the word appears to have a vast array of popular meanings, some of which accentuate the process by which new things are created from the deconstruction and reappropriation of other things. See *Urban Dictionary*, http://www.urbandictionary.com/define.php?term=mash up.

13. For a description of Coleman's evolution as a musician and his theory, see Mike Zwerin, "Ornette Coleman and the Power of Harmolodics: Learning the Repertoire," *New York Times*, September 19, 2001, http://www.nytimes.com/2001/09/19/style/19iht-zwer19_ed2_.html. Coleman's "The Harmolodic Manifesto" (n.d.) is available online, at Coleman's official Web site, http://www.ornettecoleman.com/course.swf. On Ulmer's and Reid's adoption of Coleman's philosophy and musical collaboration, see Geoffrey Himes, "James 'Blood' Ulmer and Vernon Reid: Harmolodic Blues," *JazzTimes,* July–August 2006, http://jazztimes.com/articles/17056-james-blood-ulmer-and-vernon-reid-harmolodic-blues.

14. Coleman, "Harmolodic Manifesto."

15. James Cone, *The Spirituals and the Blues: An Interpretation* (1972; repr., New York: Orbis, 2001).

16. This, he later learned, was James Blood Ulmer's, "Take My Music Back to the Church," from the CD *Birthright* (Hyena Records, 2005).

17. Using the model proposed by Judy Fentress-Williams in her commentary on Exodus for *The Africana Bible* (ed. Hugh R. Page Jr. et al. [Minneapolis: Fortress Press, 2010], 80–81), Psalm 18 and 2 Samuel 22 could be said to exist in a theologically and canonically discursive relationship in which one continually "remixes" the other.

18. On African and African-Diasporan textile traditions, see Thompson, *Flash of the Spirit,* 208–22. On the specifics of African American quilting, see Maude Wahlman, "Quilts, African American," in *Africana: The Encyclopedia of the African and African American Experience*, ed. K. Anthony Appiah and Henry Louis Gates Jr., 2nd ed. (New York: Oxford University Press, 2005).

19. This is an idea advanced by William F. Albright, "A Catalogue of Early Hebrew Lyric Poems (Psalm 68)," *Hebrew Union College Annual* 23, no. 1 (1950–51):1–39.

20. Mitchell Dahood, *Psalms II: 51–100*, vol. 17 of *The Anchor Bible,* ed. W. F. Albright and D. N. Freedman (Garden City, NY: Doubleday, 1968), 133.

PART III

Preaching, Teaching, and Living Early Hebrew Poems

Early Hebrew Poetry
Engaging It in Africana Congregational Settings

For many years now, I've had the opportunity to talk about early Hebrew poetry in various church settings, to audiences lay and ordained, within and beyond the confines of the Black church. One goal of such presentations has been to expose people to some of the more important scholarship on poetry in ancient Israel while at the same time helping them see the unique place occupied by a subset of poems considered by some to be among the Bible's most ancient texts. More recently, I have been careful to establish a context for such study that notes the source of my interest in the topic and my place within a lineage of scholars who have engaged in such work. I also invite those present directly into the conversation about the various ways in which poetry can be defined and what dynamics—biological, social, political, and religious—appear to drive it. Although the ensuing dialogue is almost always vigorous, one of the odd challenges I have had to navigate is how to frame the conversation in ways that honor the particularities of Africana life, especially in the Americas. Doing so is crucial if any of this information is to be at all valuable for teaching, preaching, spiritual direction, or the cure of souls.

From a methodological standpoint, any examination of early Hebrew poetry, whether in a scholarly or a parochial setting, is best undertaken within the parameters of the study of Hebrew poetry in general. Mundane issues such as the distinction between poetry, prose, and verse; the artistic conventions distinctive to ancient Israel; and the importance that parallelism has played in the interpretation of Hebrew poetry have to be addressed. Others, such as the impact of poetic theory on definitions of poetry; the selection of literary texts with which to compare Hebrew poetry; the impulses that might generate verse and their bearing on poetry as a genre, as well as its possible antecedents;[1] and the role that biblical scholarship has played in determining which texts are classified and presented as poetry in critical editions of the Hebrew Bible, such as *Biblia Hebraica Stuttgartensia* and in English translations such as the King James Version, the Revised Standard Version, the New Revised Standard Version, the New International Version, the Common English Bible, and others, have to be engaged as well.

Exposure to definitions of poetry from literary and biblical studies is important.[2] In addition, some exposure to the vast secondary literature on Hebrew poetry is necessary. Much can be gained from a review of Robert Lowth's legendary *Lectures on the Sacred Poetry of the Hebrews* (1787);[3] Hermann Gunkel's form-critical reflections and musings on Israelite myth and poetry in his several major works;[4] James Muilenburg's formulation of "rhetorical criticism";[5] the work of Frank Moore Cross Jr. and David Noel Freedman—both singly and in collaboration—on early Hebrew poetry and prosody;[6] and that of James Kugel on Hebrew poetry.[7] The work of Owen Barfield on verse and consciousness and that of Sherwin Nuland on poetry and embodiment also promises to shed light on poetry's mysterious origins and powers.[8]

In Africana settings, traditional biblical scholarship, whether produced by Africana or other authors, should be in direct conversation with artifacts from Africa and the African Diaspora. In the case of biblical poetry, such literary sources can readily be found, for example, in anthologies of African, Caribbean, and African American literature.[9] With regard to early Hebrew poetry, African American spirituals; blues music, poetry, and criticism; Africana literatures born of social and political resistance; and research on Black folk traditions are particularly meaningful dialogue partners.[10] Although the precise outcomes of an encounter between the First Testament, mainstream Bible scholarship, and the Africana imaginary cannot be predicted, one likely result is a deeper appreciation of the relationship between trauma and deeply evocative modes of human expression in the so-called biblical world and our own.

Poems—Hebrew or Africana, ancient or modern—are *made* things. They adhere to their own norms. The same can be said of individuals, societies, denominations, parishes, and ministries, all of which conform to their own canons.[11] An Africana engagement with early Hebrew verse, a body of tradition that purports to come from Israel's formative period, opens the door to consideration of those dynamics—physiological, social, religious, and spiritual—that generate human creativity in crisis. Prayerful consideration of such poetry, if undertaken in a manner that allows the experiences of once-colonized and -subjugated peoples of African descent to be the starting point for hermeneutical engagement, sets the stage for a poetics of liberation and spiritualities of resistance to be fashioned from Scripture, Africana traditions, and lived Black experience. It promises to enrich those spiritualities that are already part of the Africana mainstream[12] and creates room for the development of others, such as those derived from either blues traditions (such as classical, hoodoo, and harmolodic) or esoteric customs at home in Africa or the Black Diaspora. A more diverse set of tools will, of course, need to be offered to those hoping to read biblical poems, especially those poems considered to be among the First Testament's most ancient. There will be a need for works like those of James Geary, Robert McDowell, and Margaret McGee, which celebrate and offer comparable instruction on Africana poetry and poetics, that enable readers to deploy more readily such modes of discourse in talking with and responding to the poems.[13] There will also need to be a persuasive case made for critical reflection on resistance as trope in the Bible and in Africana life. This may be tough to do at a time when the so-called gospel of prosperity is enjoying such tremendous popularity. However, acts of intolerance and incivility may fuel interest in theologies that provide sustenance for hard times and power to work for positive change in an environment that remains, at times, hostile to such interventions. New opportunities and locations may also need to be found for reading and thinking about texts that subvert oppressive power structures. Perhaps the pulpit, sanctuary, and prayer meeting are no longer inclusive enough for such work. Maybe we need conversations of a radically inclusive nature about the God who makes women griots and prophets (Exodus 15; Judges 5); whose unpredictable tempests alter physical and geopolitical landscapes (Psalm 29); whose signifying and inspired whisperers hold a fragmented community together (Genesis 49; Deuteronomy 32, 33); who provides *àshe* for those on the march toward freedom (Numbers 23–24); who heals Black bodies and raises troubling questions about the persistence of patriarchy (1 Samuel 2); and who offers a harmolodic paradigm for thinking about the tragedy of war, personal empowerment, justice, the poor, and the journey we daily undertake (2 Samuel 1, 22, 23; and Psalms 68, 72, and 78).

Notes

1. Here, I've had a long-standing suspicion that the genre's headwaters might well include incantations and oracular utterances, that is, power-infused words used for transformational purposes.

2. For example, one could begin with the definition by T. Brogan in *The New Princeton Encyclopedia of Poetry and Poetics*, which describes poetry as "an instance of verbal art, a text set in verse, bound speech" ("Poetry," in *The New Princeton Encyclopedia of Poetry and Poetics*, ed. Alex Preminger and T. V. F. Brogan [Princeton, NJ: Princeton University Press, 1993], 938). One

should also consider the perspectives of others such as David Noel Freedman, for whom "prose and poetry are basically two different ways of using language," each with its own "rules of operation" (*Pottery, Poetry, and Prophecy: Collected Essays on Hebrew Poetry* [Winona Lake, IN: Eisenbrauns, 1980], 2). One should also note the now-classic views of Robert Alter, who adopts Barbara Herrnstein Smith's psychologically based definition of poetry as discourse composed of a "verbal sequence" with a "sustained rhythm" that has a consistent and intentional structure (*The Art of Biblical Poetry* [New York: Basic Books, 1985], 6); and of James Kugel, *The Idea of Biblical Poetry* (1981; repr., Baltimore, MD: Johns Hopkins University Press, 1998).

3. Robert Lowth, *Lectures on the Sacred Poetry of the Hebrews,* 2nd ed., vol. 1, ed. B. Fabian et al., Anglistica and Americana 43 (1787; repr., Hildesheim, Ger.: Olms Verlag, 1969).

4. Hermann Gunkel, *What Remains of the Old Testament and Other Essays,* trans. A. K. Dallas (New York: Macmillan, 1928); *The Legends of Genesis: The Biblical Saga and History,* trans. W. H. Carruth, repr. of the introduction to the author's *Commentary on Genesis* (1901) (New York: Schocken , 1964); *The Folktale in the Old Testament,* ed. J. W. Rogerson, trans. M. D. Rutter, Historic Texts and Interpreters in Biblical Scholarship (1917; repr., Sheffield, UK: Almond, 1987). Also see Hermann Gunkel, ed., *The Psalms: A Form-Critical Introduction,* ed. J. Reumann, trans. T. M. Horner, Facet Books Biblical Series 19 (Philadelphia: Fortress Press, 1967). Gunkel remains a fascinating figure in the history of biblical studies. His conclusion about our ability to write a history of Hebrew literature remains as true today as it was when he penned it, in the early 1900s: "Down to the present time there is, properly speaking, nothing that can be called a history of Hebrew literature, although much valuable preliminary work has been done" (*What Remains of the Old Testament,* 57). Gunkel's sense that such a history should have "little concern with the personality of the writers" and should "occupy itself more with the literary type that lies deeper than any individual effort" (59) is intriguing. Arising, as it did, from his belief that literary forms are popular constructs that express the "national genius" of a people (64), that reflect specific historical and cultural circumstances, and that give voice to important aspects of a nation's "spiritual life" (67), this idea allows one to see why he is classed as a scholar more interested in typical literary phenomena. However, there is within Gunkel's thought a dual trajectory that points toward potentially fruitful critical and interpretive endeavors. The first has to do with his interest in "the mentality and the work" (65) of the ancient "Poets, Story-tellers," and "Prophets" who made use of the many popularly created literary genres (64). The second has to do with the development of what he called an "artistic sense," which attempts "to dissect understandingly the beauty" present in Hebrew literature. Particularly heartening is his view that such work has scholarly integrity and should not be ignored as "unscientific" and "left to 'popular' writers" (61). Gunkel is, in many respects, an artist seeking to understand ancient Hebrew poetics.

5. Muilenburg's programmatic statement of this method is as follows: "What I am interested in, above all, is in understanding the nature of Hebrew literary composition, in exhibiting the structural patterns that are employed for the fashioning of a literary unit, whether in poetry or in prose, and in discerning the many and various devices by which the predications are formulated and ordered into a unified whole. Such an enterprise I should describe as rhetoric and the methodology as rhetorical criticism." "Form Criticism and Beyond," *Journal of Biblical Literature* 88 (1969): 8.

6. See, for example, Frank Moore Cross, *Canaanite Myth and Hebrew Epic: Essays in the History of the Religion of Israel* (Cambridge, MA: Harvard University Press, 1973); "Studies in the Structure of Hebrew Verse: The Prosody of Lamentations 1:1-22," in *The Word of the Lord Shall Go Forth: Essays in Honor of David Noel Freedman,* ed. Carol L. Meyers and M. O'Connor (Winona Lake, IN: Eisenbrauns, 1983); *From Epic to Canon* (Baltimore, MD: Johns Hopkins University Press, 1998); Freedman, *Pottery, Poetry, and Prophecy*; and Frank Moore Cross and David Noel Freedman, *Early Hebrew Orthography,* ed. J. B. Pritchard, American Oriental Series 36 (New Haven, CT: American Oriental Society, 1952); *Studies in Ancient Yahwistic Poetry,* 2nd ed., Biblical Resource Series (Grand Rapids, MI: Eerdmans, 1997).

7. Kugel, *Idea of Biblical Poetry*; and James Kugel, *The Great Poems of the Bible* (New York: Free Press, 1999).

8. Owen Barfield, *Poetic Diction: A Study in Meaning*, 2nd ed. (1952; repr., Middletown, CT: Wesleyan University Press, 1973); Sherwin Nuland, *The Wisdom of the Body* (New York: Knopf, 1997), 367.

9. See, respectively, Gerald Moore and Ulli Beier, eds., *The Penguin Book of Modern African Poetry*, 5th ed. (New York: Penguin, 2007); Stewart Brown and Mark McWatt, eds., *The Oxford Book of Caribbean Verse* (Oxford: Oxford University Press, 2005); and Henry Louis Gates Jr. and Nellie Y. McKay, eds., *The Norton Anthology of African American Literature* (New York: Norton, 1997).

10. See Nicole Beaulieu Herder and Ronald Herder, eds., *Best-Loved Negro Spirituals: Complete Lyrics to 178 Songs of Faith* (Mineola, NY: Dover, 2001); Junior Wells, *Hoodoo Man Blues* (expanded ed.), Delmark Records, 2011, compact disc; Ishmael Reed, *Conjure* (Amherst: University of Massachusetts Press, 1972); James Cone, *The Spirituals and the Blues: An Interpretation* (1972; repr., New York: Orbis, 2001); LeRoi Jones, *Blues People: The Negro Experience in America and the Music That Developed from It* (New York: Morrow, 1963); Frantz Fanon, *The Wretched of the Earth* (New York: Grove, 2005); Zora Neale Hurston, *Mules and Men* (1935; repr., New York: HarperPerennial, 1990).

11. This is a point stressed in my presentation for the 2005 Todd Lectures delivered at Memphis Theological Seminary in 2005. See Hugh R. Page Jr., "Performance as Interpretive Metaphor: The Bible as Libretto for Research, Translation, Preaching, and Spirituality in the Twenty-First Century; Prolegomenon," and "Performance as Interpretive Metaphor: The Bible as Libretto for Research, Translation, Preaching, and Spirituality in the Twenty-First Century; Moving from Theory to Praxis," *Memphis Theological Seminary Journal* 41 (2005): 11–33 and 34–56 respectively.

12. Robert M. Franklin's sevenfold taxonomy of African American traditions is a useful point of reference. See *Another Day's Journey: Black Churches Confronting the American Crisis* (Minneapolis: Fortress Press, 1997), 41–43.

13. James Geary, *The World in a Phrase: A Brief History of the Aphorism* (New York: Bloomsbury, 2005); Robert McDowell, *Using Poetry as Spiritual Practice: Reading, Writing, and Using Poetry in Your Daily Rituals, Aspirations, and Intentions* (New York: Free Press, 2008); Margaret D. McGee, *Haiku—the Sacred Art: A Spiritual Practice in Three Lines* (Woodstock, VT: Skylight Paths, 2009).

11

Recovering Poetry as Way of Life in the Africana World, the Church, and Beyond

Poets and poetry play a crucial role in many Africana cultures. It has even been suggested that an appreciation of the power of words and the artful use of them are features commonly shared by peoples of African descent throughout the world.[1] Poetry has also been a crucial, if somewhat underappreciated, part of the church as well. Owing in part to the ecstatic visionaries and literati that figured so prominently in the evolution of both Judaism and Christianity, poetry has long been critical to both traditions. The Tanak is filled with it. Examples are less ubiquitous, but comparably rich, in the Christian New Testament.[2] Beyond the scope of the Jewish and Christian sacred canons, there is abundant evidence of a thriving literary culture in both faith traditions that extends from early antiquity to the present.

The role of poetry and the arts is equally vital in the Black church and continues to animate Africana life today. With the global diffusion of hip-hop culture and the "spoken word" movement, poetry has become, in many ways, a twenty-first-century koine of the Africana world. Nonetheless, many consider that unique genre of "making" that is poetry to be the domain of a select few: specialists who are particularly gifted, specially graced, or professionally trained to produce it. Furthermore, in the highly specialized world of academic theology, an enterprise dominated by narrative and analytical engagement, poetry enjoys second-class status at best.[3] This marginalization represents a tacit turning away from the wellsprings of a tradition whose headwaters include the creative work of Ephrem of Edessa and other notables. Whether this trend can—or should—be reversed, and the role that Christian parishes might have in so doing, remains to be seen.

An illustrative example of what might be possible can be witnessed in the story of a small publishing enterprise, Broadside Press, and a little-known Episcopal mission in Highland Park, Michigan, during the late 1970s. Broadside was the brainchild of poet Dudley Randall. It was established to promote the work of Black authors. It served as a venue for notables such as Don L. Lee (Haki Madhubuti), Gwendolyn Brooks, Margaret Walker, Etheridge Knight, Audre Lorde, and others.[4] Having fallen on hard times in the 1970s, Randall sold the press to what was at that time an experimental congregation in the Episcopal Diocese of Michigan: the Alexander Crummell Memorial Center for Worship and Learning, in Highland Park.[5] Its administrative and distribution center was located in the building's undercroft. Its mission was closely aligned with that of the congregation, the center of whose life was a creative Eucharistic liturgy that melded Christian theology with the *nguzo saba* ("seven principles") of Kwanzaa. At its zenith, the church was also home to an independent school for community children.[6]

In 1984, I served for a brief time as interim vicar of Alexander Crummell. Both the congregation and the press were magnets for those seeking an environment in which the entire sweep of Africana life could be brought into sustained dialogue with Christian faith. It was a hub for cultural and political activities. In more than three decades of ordained ministry, I have been affiliated with no other congregation that was as successful in bringing Africana expressive culture and spirituality together in such a nurturing matrix. To read, think about, and interpret Scripture in this context required awareness of how Black life was impacted by the urban and industrial challenges facing Detroit in the 1980s and the economic difficulties confronting its Black residents. The congregation lived up to its name as a "center" whose worship and cultural initiatives, including Broadside Press, honored Africana life and promoted creative engagement of it.[7] Poetry was, at least for a time, wired into the institutional DNA of the place.

The Bible's most ancient poems and the Africana world have important things to say to one another. Unfortunately, the conversation between the two is capable of taking place only in settings that permit each to speak with clarity and candor. Given some of the "baggage" each brings to such an encounter, it is not surprising that the church—and the Black church in particular—has proven to be a less-than-congenial location in which to have such a conversation. Early Hebrew poems and the Africana world are the domain of powerful women, inscrutable tempests, signifiers and whisperers, conjurers, asymmetrical reversals, and esoteric mash-ups. In the most optimal of circumstances, an encounter of eschatological scope involving the two would be possible, one that allowed deep communion between Africana readers, the poems, and the ineffable divine force whose *àshe* is revealed therein. An approach leading to such an end should be at once reverent, receptive, and mischievous. It should take place in an intellectual space akin to the Canaanite highlands where a multicultural multitude of displaced peoples appears to have become a confederation under the divine patronage of YHWH (Exod. 12:38);[8] in the "hush arbors" and "praise houses" where enslaved Africans in the southern United States preserved, and in some cases recast, rituals and lore from Africa; and in the "juke joints" and nightclubs in which blues musicians fashioned a cosmos where Louisiana was sacred ground and where "mojos" and "dusted brooms" could change the course of history.

Becoming such a welcoming place where the Africana world and early Hebrew poems can meet should be one of the church's highest priorities. Prayerful consideration of the major themes these poems raise offers a starting point for this process. How might this be done? The poems can certainly be read individually.[9] Another approach is to cluster and read them according to organizational themes and structures derived from Africana life. This has been the method employed in this book. A third model involves applying interpretive paradigms that mirror or mimic Africana expressive tropes to contemplate and converse with them.

One such approach, poetic responses, is presented here. Its intent is to complement the seven "readings" of early Hebrew poetry encountered thus far. The verse form used is based on the number symbolism of Willie Dixon's classic song "Hoochie Coochie Man."[10] Its prosodic structure takes its inspiration from the number of rhythmic beats—five in total: "da-da-da-da-da"—in the riff that opens each of the song's verses. Its three five-syllable lines call to mind the *àshe* that odd numbers appear to possess in African American conjure.

Exodus 15
Jah's women not seen
Alone and unheard
Let us not forget.

—

Judges 5
In times of crisis
Hospitality
Freedom's door opens.

—

Psalm 29

Storms and crashing waves
Raging, tearing down
God's great paradox.

—

Genesis 49 • Deuteronomy 32, 33
Signify, whisper
Sew into the *quilt*
Hope—*nkisi* dreams.

—

Numbers 23–24
Conjure with clear sight
Know the limits Love
Has set for *àshe.*

—

1 Samuel 2
Black bodies—broken
Raise, restore, unchain
Prison bars destroy.

—

2 Samuel 1, 22, 23; Psalms 68, 72, 78
Hidden in plain sight
A *creole mash-up*
Our *nsibidi.*

Such experimental readings are of value to both biblical studies and theology, insofar as the particularities of Africana existence, when brought into dialogue with the milieu that witnessed Israel's birth, provide insight into some of the dynamics that shape social life and impact mythopoesis, the creation of myths. Such interpretive engagements also promise to bring early Hebrew poems into a more responsible and critical dialogue with archeological data in a conversation that does not have to presume either the historical veracity of events described in the First Testament or the antiquity of the sources preserving such lore. Instead, given the paucity and disputed nature of controls to establish date and provenance of most biblical traditions, this conversation allows certain texts, or aggregates thereof, to be interpreted in light of multiple data sets (archeological, literary, and anthropological among them) and by utilizing an array of methods particularly suited to the synthesizing of information drawn from different kinds of artifacts.[11]

Notes

1. See, for example, Dale Andrews's assessment in "Black Preaching Praxis," in *Black Church Studies: An Introduction*, ed. S. Floyd-Thomas et al. (Nashville, TN: Abingdon, 2007), 207–8.

2. A few poignant examples are Luke 1:46-55, 68-79; 2:29-31; 1 Corinthians 13; Phil. 2:6-11; and perhaps the one-word "maranatha" prayer (1 Cor. 16:22; Rev. 22:20), which Oscar Cullman identified as an ancient Christian liturgical formula; see his *Early Christian Worship* (Norwich, UK: SCM, 1953), 13.

3. This is something that Richard Viladesau seeks to address by arguing that the theological enterprise should not be treated "as a separate sphere, separate from and complementary to the aesthetic domain of Christian existence, but as one that overlaps with the latter substantially, both in content and in form." See *Theology and the Arts: Encountering God through Music, Art, and Rhetoric* (Mahwah, NJ: Paulist, 2000), 4.

4. Julius Thompson, *Dudley Randall, Broadside Press, and the Black Arts Movement in Detroit, 1960–1995* (Jefferson, NC: McFarland, 1999), 1.

5. On Randall, see Kate Tuttle, "Randall, Dudley Felker," in *Africana: The Encyclopedia of the African and African American Experience*, ed. Kwame Anthony Appiah and Henry Louis Gates Jr., 2nd ed. (New York: Oxford University Press. 2005). On Broadside Press, see "Broadside Press Publications, Detroit, Michigan" (http://clarke.cmich.edu/resource_tab/ bibliographies_of_clarke_library_material/broadside_press_of_detroit/ broadside_press_of_detroit_index.html), Clarke Historical Library, Central Michigan University, June 1, 2012. On the relationship between Randall, Broadside, and the Alexander Crummell Memorial Center for Worship and Learning, see J. Thompson, *Dudley Randall*, 133–80, 193, 245.

6. In 2005, that school celebrated three decades of continuous service. For a profile of it, see "Detroit's Oldest African-Centered School Celebrates 30 Years and a Broader Vision for the Future," *Michigan Citizen*, June 26, 2005, http://michigancitizen.com/detroits-oldest-african-centered-school-celebrates-30-years-and-a-broader-vision-for-the-future/.

7. For a brief treatment of the work of the priest responsible for establishing and leading this effort, the Reverend Kwasi (Anthony) Thornell, see Irene Jackson-Brown, "Music among Blacks in the Episcopal Church: Some Preliminary Considerations," in *Readings in African American Church Music and Worship*, ed. J. Abington (Chicago: GIA, 2001), 230–31.

8. For this and comparable views of Israelite origins, see, for example, Victor Matthews and Don Benjamin, *The Social World of Ancient Israel, 1250–587 BCE* (Peabody, MA: Hendrickson, 1993), 1–5; and William G. Dever, *Who Were the Early Israelites and Where Did They Come From?* (Grand Rapids, MI: Eerdmans, 2003), 194–208.

9. This is the approach taken in one of my earlier studies, "Toward the Creation of Transformational Spiritualities: Re-Engaging Israel's Early Poetic Tradition in Light of the Church's Preferential Option for the Poor," in *The Option for the Poor in Christian Theology*, ed. D. Groody (Notre Dame, IN: University of Notre Dame Press, 2007).

10. The various versions of this song made famous by McKinley Morganfield (Muddy Waters) are used as points of reference. Of the aforementioned, track 5 on the CD *Hoochie Coochie Man* (Just a Memory Records, 1999) is particularly illustrative of the pattern described.

11. Dever's treatment of the Exodus and Moses traditions reflects such a nuanced approach (*Who Were the Early Israelites?*, 232–37).

Conclusion: Early Hebrew Poetry and Spiritualities of Resistance in the Black Atlantic

Study of the theologies implicitly and explicitly articulated in early Hebrew poetry, and the ways in which Jews, Christians, and others have responded to them, continues to have currency today. Considered within the context of the Christian Bible, early Hebrew poems are particularly useful in developing parameters for twenty-first-century Africana spiritualities of resistance and hope. A natural outgrowth of reading them prayerfully and reflecting on their themes and placement within the canon is a renewed appreciation for the power of poetry in daily life and the theological potential of social marginalization. A discipline that treats these poems as a special literary collection within a larger biblical anthology and that promotes the reading of them as exercises in an Ignatian sense can perhaps heighten awareness of the sacred and can help Africana people of faith read the Bible carefully, probe its meaning deeply, and use it in ways that strengthen bonds within and beyond the Africana community. Of particular concern is what promise these early poems might hold for those seeking to live full and meaningful lives of faith while countering the long-term effects of racism, discrimination, the AIDS crisis, family dissolution, the erosion of trust in Black institutions, political instability and genocide in Africa, and various other crises that are affecting Africana peoples worldwide.

THE PERIODIZATION OF EARLY HEBREW: A DIASPORAN STORY

David Noel Freedman's historical periodization for early Hebrew poems offers an interesting starting point for thinking about crises confronting early Israel as well as for thinking about women and men living in the Africana world, namely, militant Mosaic Yahwism (twelfth century BCE; Exodus 15; Psalm 29; Judges 5); patriarchal revival (eleventh century BCE; Genesis 49; Numbers 23–24; Deuteronomy 33); and monarchic syncretism (tenth century BCE; 1

Samuel 2; 2 Samuel 1; 2 Samuel 23; 2 Samuel 22 (= Psalm 18); Deuteronomy 32; Psalms 78, 68, 72). This schema suggests some important things about the evolution of religious ideas in early Israel. It shows us how an ethnically diverse community formed a religiously based social charter centered on common belief in a divine sovereign. It illustrates how the people wrestled, over time, with the implications of their mixed ancestry and with their various and, at times, competing conceptions of God and cultural mores. It makes clear the ways in which they blended their traditions into a "creolized diasporan hybrid" that was fluid and adaptable to changing social and political needs. It is, in a real sense, the tale of a diasporan people whose historical memories tie them to at least three homelands—Mesopotamia, Egypt, and Canaan—with which their relations are at times strained. It is a community that experienced flight and reformation while dealing as best it could with the mysteries of suffering, rebirth, tragedy, and grace.

In sum, these poems tell a moving story of a community born in crisis; faced with a legacy of oppression; seeking independence and interdependence; heterogeneous rather than homogeneous in social makeup; struggling to articulate its understanding of the divine while at the same time defining itself; utilizing creative and at times countercultural strategies to survive; and relying heavily on wordsmiths—poets, prophets, and sages—as its mediators and spokespersons. These inspired individuals knew their constituencies well and challenged them to reflect in ways that many of us today find jarring and inappropriate. They mince no words when talking about life's triumphs, tragedies, and ambiguities. They are unafraid to talk about God's power to liberate as well as the Lord's inscrutable ways. They raise difficult and at times unanswerable questions, such as, Who is my neighbor? What should our relationship to the ancestors be? How can we be at one and the same time unified and independent as members of a community? Does the Almighty stand by those of us who are neither wealthy nor influential? Is not war, though at times a necessity, inevitably tragic? Does just behavior, by both ordinary folk and those in positions of public trust, truly yield positive and measurable outcomes? What is required to be a good steward of cultural traditions and practices? Are the margins, the sidelines, the backwater regions, really places that God cares about? These poets—and the editors responsible for bringing together their work and placing it strategically within the canon of the Tanak—knew that, in both the public arena and the private sphere, their inspired musings would be the start of many conversations. They saw in such exchanges, however disconcerting, a necessary component for building community.

CROSSING THE HISTORICAL DIVIDE

The picture we get from Early Hebrew poems is of a community facing challenges not unlike some of those faced by Africana peoples globally—a community experiencing perennial crisis, facing and attempting to make peace with a history of oppression, striving for independence and interdependence, heterogeneous in constitution, continually articulating (and rearticulating) its understanding of the divine and itself, utilizing at times transgressive strategies to deal with life's difficulties, and relying heavily on griots—poets, musicians, priests, pastors, and public officials—as spokespersons. Looking specifically at African Americans, we are part of a complex matrix encompassing Africa and the many regions around the world to which Africans have been carried forcibly, to which they have migrated voluntarily, or to which they have fled as a result of persecution. From the standpoint of both the African continental and Black-Diasporan experiences, the Atlantic slave trade and European colonial activity are perhaps the most important factors that have shaped, and continue to impact, the Africana ethos worldwide. Finally, many scholars have noted that life in the African Diaspora has been, and remains, characterized by alienation, isolation, and ontological crisis generated by contested identities and epistemologies. Furthermore, Africana peoples continue to have an ongoing, if at times problematic, relationship with Scripture. We approach it from various perspectives, each of which is influenced by an enormous number of factors. Some of the more obvious are the theologies of our respective faith communities; popular and prevailing attitudes about the Bible; received cultural traditions about how the Bible is to be read; and personal attitudes about sacred texts in general. No one, therefore, can claim to read the Bible without applying some set of presuppositions. Discerning what those notions are, charting them, and asking what such ideas tell us about ourselves and Africana life are essential first steps for engaging early Hebrew poems and other passages of Scripture. Most readers have favorite verses, chapters, books, or sections of the Bible. A few even have a particular testament (Old/First or New/Second) to which they feel a particular kinship. These preferences are usually developed over time as one hears Scripture read in worship or in private devotional encounters. Such passages become our canon within the overall canon. They become trusted friends to whom we turn in times of crisis or when in need of special inspiration. Some people mark them with ribbons or highlight them with brightly colored pens so they can be easily located when needed. This strategy makes a difficult and at times unwieldy holy anthology manageable. It allows one to stake a claim on the Bible and establish a personal vantage point from which to survey the entire scriptural landscape.

TOWARD AN INTEGRATIVE AND SCRIPTURAL AFRICANA SPIRITUALITY OF RESISTANCE

When we consider that fragmented communities and obliterated selves are the pieces from which enslaved Africans in the New World assembled a cosmos and a life, and that the Bible and other religious texts have been sources of both stability and instability within Africana communities, readers have a responsibility to be historically well informed, socially conscious, and theologically sophisticated as they read and appropriate the Bible—particularly within faith communities. Thus, further consideration ought to be given to some of the following implications of early Hebrew poetry for Africana life today. First, these poems remind us that our lives as peoples of Africa and the African Diaspora are inspired assemblages of artifacts, memories, and dreams. They must be cherished, passed on, interpreted, and at times adapted for future generations. Second, they caution us that the life of the spirit in Africana communities involves prayerfully taking on several functions, such as collector, curator, steward, and interpreter. All bring with them the responsibility of being attentive to the past (origins), present (current circumstances / social context), and future (dreams/aspirations)—both of individuals and of the community as a whole. Third, these poems suggest to us that from a Christian perspective, Africana spirituality might best be seen as a holistic, fully embodied, and theologically grounded response to, and examination of, the Africana experience worldwide. Thus, Africana readers cannot afford to be narrowly parochial in their orientation or efforts to reach out and build community. Fourth, early Hebrew poems teach us that life's tragedies, contradictions, and ambiguities must not be ignored. They are the rough edges of Africana life that cannot—and should not—be sanded down by facile theological reflection and constructive efforts. Fifth, members of the Africana community should strive to become fully conversant with Africana expressive culture. The arts—visual, literary, musical, and plastic—are needed to glimpse the transcendent and are invaluable in charting our journey with and toward God. Sixth, this body of ancient biblical poems shows us that polyphony, descant, and theological "note bending" typify the day-to-day experience of peoples whose lives are touched in any way by sociopolitical and/or religious marginalization. Africana spiritualities need to embrace this fact as an asset rather than viewing it as a liability. Seventh, these poems demonstrate very clearly that transgression, agglutination, testing, and synthesis are tools that can be used creatively in Africana identity construction and community building. Early Israelites appear to have been quite daring and experimental in their use of God talk and in their development of both forms of governance and religious ritual. They tested ideas, brought together elements that appeared at first to be incongruous, and made their own new amalgams. This is a well-known aspect of Africana life that must not be lost. Eighth, we learn that words, skillfully deployed, hold the power to harm, heal, restore, and create. They can be building blocks in fashioning an inclusive and welcoming *communitas Africana* globally. We need to appreciate their potential and train ourselves to use them prudently. Finally, early Hebrew poetry reminds us that the poet is a mediator of eschatological convergence. The making of a poem is a sacred act. Within Africana contexts, the creation and sharing of poetry should be seen as acts of generosity with the potential to shed light on who and what we are as individuals: threads in an interdependent web consisting of all peoples, and citizens of a global community.

As for the role of the Africana Bible scholar who also happens to be a cleric or lay leader within the Black church, perhaps there is some utility in using the medial ministry of the Ethiopian *dabtara* as one of many models for those who provide the intellectual and spiritual energy for an Africana hermeneutic that is liberating and empowering. The *dabtara* assumes, among other roles, those of intuitive, healer, singer, artist, amulet maker, steward of secret lore, and custodian of traditions. Those embracing the model of the *dabtara* would, therefore, commit themselves to encounters with early Hebrew poems, the Bible as a whole, and other traditions acknowledged as mediators of power that are restorative.[1] Perhaps such subversion of the normative practices of the biblical exegete will offer one means to follow the lead of Vincent Wimbush and undo the damage done by the uncritical embrace or oppressive use of any text or interpretive medium, to escape what he terms "the slavery that is scripturalization";[2] or a way of adopting Houston Baker's understanding of blues as "matrix" as well as "code and force" and applying them—following his inspiration—to "translate" and "train" the at-times fraught and contested byways of the academy and the church—not as an intellectual "hobo" but as Black cosmopolitan *boho* (bohemian).[3]

Early Hebrew poetry gives us ready access to the spiritual musings of some of our ancient Jewish spiritual forebears. It takes us to the fountainhead of the Judeo-Christian tradition, the root from which the branches of Second Temple Judaism, Christianity, and Islam would later grow. It brings us face-to-face with the intractable mysteries surrounding the formation of community. It shows us the role that poets and poetic language played in shaping our conceptions of the divine and our understanding of how God's self-disclosure to humanity unfolds. It forces us to deal with the symbolic nature of theological and poetic language and asks that we stretch ourselves intellectually as people of faith. It forces us to search for the common ground—to use a term often employed by African American mystic Howard Thurman[4]—on which all humans stand. It helps us to look within the biblical text, the traditions that shaped and preserved it in its various Jewish and Christian versions, and ourselves for the eternal fire of love about which the Song of Songs speaks (8:6-8). It has the potential to be a modern impetus for building a global Africana community that realizes in full measure the dreams of W. E. B. DuBois and countless others who labored to lay its foundations. These poems can be all of these things to us, and so much more, if only we would read them prayerfully and well.

Notes

1. On the training, ambiguous status, and various functions of the *dabtara*, see Jacques Mercier, *Ethiopian Magic Scrolls* (New York: Braziller, 1979), 15–28; and *Art That Heals: The Image as Medicine in Ethiopia* (New York: Museum of Modern Art and Prestel-Verlag, 1997), 41–61. Edward Hays most closely approximates such work, on the popular level, in his *The Ethiopian Tattoo Shop* (Leavenworth, KS: Forest of Peace, 1983), 166–69.

2. Vincent Wimbush, *White Men's Magic: Scripturalization as Slavery* (New York: Oxford, 2012): 233.

3. Houston A. Baker Jr., *Blues, Ideology, and Afro-American Literature* (Chicago: University of Chicago Press, 1984), 3–6, 7, 8.

4. Howard Thurman, *The Search for Common Ground: An Inquiry into the Basis of Man's Experience of Community* (1973; repr., Richmond, IN: Friends United, 2000).

Blues Note: A Poetic Afterword

Flatted thirds and muted fifths
Blue notes on poems
Born in crisis
Performed
Preserved
Pondered
Through endless years
Overture for Africana librettos
Continental, Diasporan, born of *Blacksouls*.

———

Not everyone's cup of tea
Self-absorption serving few
No *enduring* value
Random
Rambling
Reason?
Set captives *free*
Give silenced *voices* speech
Conjure a people hopeful, dreaming.

———

Liberating praxis this discordant riff
Whatever cost or backlash
Fear is vanquished
Ma'afa
Diaspora
Jah Love
Open doors all
Ways from *no way*
Paths *around* texts to freedom.

Bibliography

Albright, William F. "Archeology Confronts Biblical Criticism." *American Scholar* 7, no. 2 (1938) 176–88.

———. "A Catalogue of Early Hebrew Lyric Poems (Psalm 68)." *Hebrew Union College Annual* 23, no. 1 (1950–51):1–39.

Alter, Robert. *The Art of Biblical Poetry.* New York: Basic Books, 1985.

Althaus-Reid, Marcella. *Indecent Theology: Theological Perversions in Sex, Gender, and Politics.* London: Routledge, 2000.

Anderson, Jeffrey E. *Conjure in African American Society.* Baton Rouge: Louisiana State University Press, 2005.

———. *Hoodoo, Voodoo, and Conjure: A Handbook.* Greenwood Folklore Handbooks. Westport, CT: Greenwood, 2008.

Andrews, Dale P. "Black Preaching Praxis." In *Black Church Studies: An Introduction,* edited by S. Floyd-Thomas et al. Nashville, TN: Abingdon, 2007.

Appiah, Kwame Anthony, and Henry Louis Gates Jr., eds. *Africana: The Encyclopedia of the African and African American Experience.* 2nd ed. New York: Oxford University Press, 2005.

Attridge, Harold W., et al., eds. *The Harper Collins Study Bible.* Rev. ed. New York: HarperOne, 2006.

Baker, Houston A., Jr. *Blues, Ideology, and Afro-American Literature.* Chicago: University of Chicago Press, 1984.

Ball, Ann. *The How-To Book of Sacramentals: Everything You Need to Know but No One Ever Taught You.* Huntington, IN: Our Sunday Visitor, 2005.

Barfield, Owen. *Poetic Diction: A Study in Meaning.* 2nd ed. 1952. Reprint, Middletown, CT: Wesleyan University Press, 1973.

Bedini, Silvio. *The Life of Benjamin Banneker: The First African-American Man of Science.* 2nd ed. Baltimore: Maryland Historical Society, 1999.

Bishop, Maurice. *Forward Ever!* Sydney, Australia: Pathfinder, 1982.

"Broadside Press Publications, Detroit, Michigan" (http://clarke.cmich.edu/resource_tab/bibliographies_of_clarke_library_material/broadside_press_of_detroit/broadside_press_of_detroit_index.html). Clarke Historical Library, Central Michigan University, June 1, 2012.

Brogan, T. V. F. "Poetry." In *The New Princeton Encyclopedia of Poetry and Poetics*, edited by A. Preminger and T. V. F. Brogan. Princeton, NJ: Princeton University Press, 1993.

Brown, Stewart, and Mark McWatt, eds. *The Oxford Book of Caribbean Verse.* Oxford: Oxford University Press, 2005.

Chireau, Yvonne P. *Black Magic: Religion and the African American Conjuring Tradition.* Berkeley: University of California Press, 2003.

Coleman, Ornette. "The Harmolodic Manifesto," n.d. Coleman's official Web site. http://www.ornettecoleman.com/course.swf.

Cone, James. *The Spirituals and the Blues: An Interpretation.* 1972. Reprint, New York: Orbis, 2001.

Cross, Frank Moore. *Canaanite Myth and Hebrew Epic: Essays in the History of the Religion of Israel.* Cambridge, MA: Harvard University Press, 1973.

———. *From Epic to Canon.* Baltimore, MD: Johns Hopkins University Press, 1998.

———. "Studies in the Structure of Hebrew Verse: The Prosody of Lamentations 1:1-22." In *The Word of the Lord Shall Go Forth: Essays in Honor of David Noel Freedman*, edited by Carol L. Meyers and M. O'Connor. Winona Lake, IN: Eisenbrauns, 1983.

Cross, Frank Moore, and David Noel Freedman. *Early Hebrew Orthography.* Edited by J. B. Pritchard. American Oriental Series 36. New Haven, CT: American Oriental Society, 1952.

———. *Studies in Ancient Yahwistic Poetry.* 2nd ed. Biblical Resource Series. Grand Rapids, MI: Eerdmans, 1997.

Cullman, Oscar. *Early Christian Worship.* Norwich, UK: SCM, 1953.

Dahood, Mitchell. *Psalms II: 51–100.* Vol. 17 of *The Anchor Bible*, edited by W. F. Albright and D. N. Freedman. Garden City, NY: Doubleday, 1968.

Dalglish, Cass. *Humming the Blues.* Corvalis, OR: Calyx, 2008.

Denzin, Norman. *Interpretive Ethnography: Ethnographic Practices for the 21st Century.* Thousand Oaks, CA: Sage, 1997.

"Detroit's Oldest African-Centered School Celebrates 30 Years and a Broader Vision for the Future." *Michigan Citizen,* June 26, 2005. http://michigancitizen.com/detroits-oldest-african-centered-school-celebrates-30-years-and-a-broader-vision-for-the-future/.

Dever, William G. *The Lives of Ordinary People in Ancient Israel: Where Archaeology and the Bible Intersect.* Grand Rapids, MI: Eerdmans, 2012.

———. *Who Were the Early Israelites and Where Did They Come From?* Grand Rapids, MI: Eerdmans, 2003.

Fanon, Frantz. *The Wretched of the Earth*. New York: Grove Press, 2005.

Fentress-Williams, Judy. "Exodus." In Page et al., *Africana Bible*.

Finn, Julio. *The Bluesman: The Musical Heritage of Black Men and Women in the Americas*. New York: Interlink, 1992.

Franklin, Robert M. *Another Day's Journey: Black Churches Confronting the American Crisis*. Minneapolis: Fortress Press, 1997.

Freedman, David Noel. *Pottery, Poetry, and Prophecy: Collected Essays on Hebrew Poetry*. Winona Lake, IN: Eisenbrauns, 1980.

Gates, Henry Louis, Jr. *The Signifying Monkey: A Theory of African-American Literary Criticism*. New York: Oxford University Press, 1988.

Gates, Henry Louis, Jr., and Nellie Y. McKay, eds. *The Norton Anthology of African American Literature*. New York: Norton, 1997.

Geary, James. *The World in a Phrase: A Brief History of the Aphorism*. New York: Bloomsbury, 2005.

Ginsberg, H. L. "A Phoenician Hymn in the Psalter." 1935. In *Atti del XIX Congresso Internazionale degli Orientalisti*. Rome: Bardi, 1938.

Glassner, Jean-Jacques. "The Use of Knowledge in Ancient Mesopotamia." In *Civilizations of the Ancient Near East*, edited by J. M. Sasson. Peabody, MA: Hendrickson, 2000.

Gordon, Cyrus Herzl. *A Scholar's Odyssey*. Biblical Scholarship in North America 20. Atlanta, GA: Society of Biblical Literature, 2000.

Gumbrecht, Hans Ulrich. *The Powers of Philology: Dynamics of Textual Scholarship*. Urbana: University of Illinois Press, 2003.

Gunkel, Hermann. *The Folktale in the Old Testament*. Edited by J. W. Rogerson. Translated by M. D. Rutter. Translation of the 1917 edition. Historic Texts and Interpreters in Biblical Scholarship. Sheffield, UK: Almond, 1987.

———. *The Legends of Genesis: The Biblical Saga and History*. Translated by W. H. Carruth. Reprint of the introduction to the author's *Commentary on Genesis*, published in 1901. New York: Schocken, 1964.

———. *What Remains of the Old Testament and Other Essays*. Translated by A. K. Dallas. New York: Macmillan, 1928.

Gunkel, Hermann, ed. *The Psalms: A Form-Critical Introduction*. Edited by J. Reumann. Translated by T. M. Horner. Facet Books Biblical Series 19. Philadelphia: Fortress Press, 1967.

Hack, Serajul. *Gone . . . But Not Forgotten . . . Hurricane Ivan*. Pittsburgh: Dorrance, 2007.

Hays, Edward M. *The Ethiopian Tattoo Shop*. Leavenworth, KS: Forest of Peace, 1983.

Heine, Jorge. "The Return of Bernard Coard." *Gleaner* (Jamaica), September 20, 2009. http://jamaica-gleaner.com/gleaner/20090920/focus/focus6.html.

Herder, Nicole Beaulieu, and Ronald Herder, eds. *Best-Loved Negro Spirituals: Complete Lyrics to 178 Songs of Faith.* Mineola, NY: Dover, 2001.

Himes, Geoffrey. "James 'Blood' Ulmer and Vernon Reid: Harmolodic Blues." *JazzTimes,* July–August 2006. http://jazztimes.com/articles/17056-james-blood-ulmer-and-vernon-reid-harmolodic-blues.

Holmes, Barbara A. *Joy Unspeakable: Contemplative Practices of the Black Church.* Minneapolis: Fortress Press, 2004.

Hood, Robert. *Must God Remain Greek? Afro Cultures and God-Talk.* Minneapolis: Fortress Press, 1990.

hooks, bell. *Bone Black: Memories of Girlhood.* New York: Holt, 1996.

hooks, bell, and Cornel West. *Breaking Bread: Insurgent Black Intellectual Life.* Toronto, Ont.: Between the Lines, 1991.

Humez, Jean M. *Harriet Tubman: The Life and Life Stories.* Madison: University of Wisconsin Press, 2003.

Hurston, Zora Neale. *Moses, Man of the Mountain.* 1939. Reprint, New York: HarperPerennial, 1991.

———. *Mules and Men.* 1935. Reprint, New York: HarperPerennial, 1990.

Jackson-Brown, Irene. "Music among Blacks in the Episcopal Church: Some Preliminary Considerations." In *Readings in African American Church Music and Worship,* edited by J. Abington. Chicago: GIA, 2001.

Jones, LeRoi. *Blues People: The Negro Experience in America and the Music That Developed from It.* New York: Morrow, 1963.

Kennedy, James M. "Psalm 29 as Semiotic System: A Linguistic Reading." *Journal of Hebrew Scriptures* 9, no. 12 (2009):1–21.

Kramer, Samuel Noah. *In the World of Sumer: An Autobiography.* Detroit, MI: Wayne State University Press, 1988.

Kugel, James L. *The Great Poems of the Bible.* New York: Free Press, 1999.

———. *The Idea of Biblical Poetry.* 1981. Reprint, Baltimore, MD: Johns Hopkins University Press, 1998.

Long, Burke O. *Planting and Reaping Albright: Politics, Ideology, and Interpreting the Bible.* University Park: Pennsylvania State University Press, 1997.

Lowth, Robert. *Lectures on the Sacred Poetry of the Hebrews.* 2nd ed. Vol. 1. Edited by B. Fabian et al. 1787. Anglistica and Americana 43. Reprint, Hildesheim, Ger.: Olms Verlag, 1969.

Major, Clarence. *Juba to Jive: A Dictionary of African-American Slang.* New York: Penguin, 1994.

Mason, Eric F., Samuel I. Thomas, Alison Schofield, and Eugene Ulrich. *A Teacher for all Generations: Essays in Honor of James C. Vanderkam*. Vol. 1. Supplements to the Journal for the Study of Judaism, volume 153/1 (Leiden: Brill, 2012): 37–47.

Mason, Theodore O., Jr. "Signifying." In Appiah and Gates, *Africana*.

Matthews, Victor H., and Don C. Benjamin. *The Social World of Ancient Israel, 1250–587 BCE*. Peabody, MA: Hendrickson, 1993.

McDermott, John J. *What Are They Saying about the Formation of Israel?* What Are They Saying About Series. Mahwah, NJ: Paulist, 1998.

McDowell, Robert. *Using Poetry as Spiritual Practice: Reading, Writing, and Using Poetry in Your Daily Rituals, Aspirations, and Intentions*. New York: Free Press, 2008.

McGee, Margaret D. *Haiku—the Sacred Art: A Spiritual Practice in Three Lines*. Woodstock, VT: Skylight Paths, 2009.

Mercier, Jacques. *Art That Heals: The Image as Medicine in Ethiopia*. New York: Museum of Modern Art and Prestel-Verlag, 1997.

———. *Ethiopian Magic Scrolls*. New York: Braziller, 1979.

Mitchem, Stephanie. *African American Folk Healing*. New York: New York University Press, 2007.

Moore, Gerald, and Ulli Beier, eds. *The Penguin Book of Modern African Poetry*. 5th ed. New York: Penguin, 2007.

Muilenburg, James. "Form Criticism and Beyond." *Journal of Biblical Literature* 88 (1969): 1–18.

Nuland, Sherwin B. *The Wisdom of the Body*. New York: Knopf, 1997.

O'Connor, Kathleen. "Orishas." In Appiah and Gates, *Africana*.

O'Garro, Dorine S. *Montserrat on My Mind: Tales of Montserrat*. Bloomington: Author House, 2004.

O'Shaughnessy, Hugh. "Sir Eric Gairy" (obituary). *Independent* (London), August 25, 1997. http://www.independent.co.uk/news/people/obituary-sir-eric-gairy-1247273.html.

Oyelaran, Olasope O. "In What Tongue?" In *Orisa Devotion as World Religion: The Globalization of Yoruba Religious Culture*, edited by J. Olupona and T. Rey. Madison: University of Wisconsin Press, 2008.

Page, Hugh R., Jr. "Early Hebrew Poetry and Ancient Pre-Biblical Sources." In Page et al., *Africana Bible*.

———. "Ethnological Criticism: An Apologia and Application." In *Exploring New Paradigms in Biblical and Cognate Studies*, edited by Hugh R. Page Jr. Lewiston, NY: Mellen Biblical Press, 1996.

———. Forthcoming. "Myth and Social Realia in Ancient Israel: Early Hebrew Poems as Folkloric Assemblage." In *Myth and Scripture: Contemporary Perspectives on Religion, Language, and Imagination*, edited by J. Dexter E. Callender. Atlanta, GA: Society of Biblical Literature, 2013.

———. "Myth, Meta-Narrative, and Historical Reconstruction: Rethinking the Nature of Scholarship on Israelite Origins." In *Studies in the Hebrew Bible, Qumran, and the Septuagint Presented to Eugene Ulrich*, edited by Peter W. Flint, Emanuel Tov, and James C. VanderKam. Leiden, Neth.: Brill, 2006.

———. *The Myth of Cosmic Rebellion: A Study of Its Reflexes in Ugaritic and Biblical Literature*. Supplements to *Vetus Testamentum* 65. Leiden, Neth.: Brill, 1996.

———. "Performance as Interpretive Metaphor: The Bible as Libretto for Research, Translation, Preaching, and Spirituality in the Twenty-First Century; Prolegomenon." *Memphis Theological Seminary Journal* 41 (2005): 11–33.

———. "Performance as Interpretive Metaphor: The Bible as Libretto for Research, Translation, Preaching, and Spirituality in the Twenty-First Century; Moving from Theory to Praxis." *Memphis Theological Seminary Journal* 41 (2005): 34–56.

———. "Toward the Creation of Transformational Spiritualities: Re-Engaging Israel's Early Poetic Tradition in Light of the Church's Preferential Option for the Poor." In *The Option for the Poor in Christian Theology*, edited by D. Groody. Notre Dame, IN: University of Notre Dame Press, 2007.

Page, Hugh R., Jr., et al., eds. *The Africana Bible : Reading Israel's Scriptures from Africa and the African Diaspora*. Minneapolis, MN: Fortress Press, 2010.

Parker, Simon. "Toward Literary Translations of Ugaritic Poetry." *Ugarit-Forschungen* 22 (1990): 257–70.

Pietila, Antero. *Not in My Neighborhood: How Bigotry Shaped a Great American City*. Chicago, IL: Dee, 2010.

Reed, Ishmael. *Conjure*. Amherst: University of Massachusetts Press, 1972.

———. *Mumbo Jumbo*. 1972. Reprint, New York: Scribner, 1996.

Robinson, Lisa Clayton. "Bishop, Maurice." In Appiah and Gates, *Africana*.

Rodgers, Lawrence R. "Talented Tenth, The." In Appiah and Gates, *Africana*.

Running, Leona Glidden, and David Noel Freedman. *William Foxwell Albright: A 20th Century Genius*. 1975. Reprint, Berrien Springs, MI: Andrews University Press, 1991.

Skloot, Rebecca. *The Immortal Life of Henrietta Lacks*. New York: Crown, 2010.

Smith, Theophus. *Conjuring Culture: Biblical Formations of Black America*. New York: Oxford University Press, 1994.

Staley, Jeffrey L. *Reading with A Passion: Rhetoric, Autobiography, and the American West in the Gospel of John*. New York: Continuum, 1995.

Thompson, Julius E. *Dudley Randall, Broadside Press, and the Black Arts Movement in Detroit, 1960–1995*. Jefferson, NC: McFarland, 1999.

Thompson, Robert Farris. *Flash of the Spirit: African and Afro-American Art and Philosophy*. New York: Vintage, 1984.

Thurman, Howard. *The Search for Common Ground: An Inquiry into the Basis of Man's Experience of Community*. 1973. Reprint, Richmond, IN: Friends United, 2000.

Tuttle, Kate. "Randall, Dudley Felker." In Appiah and Gates, *Africana*.

Viladesau, Richard. *Theology and the Arts: Encountering God through Music, Art, and Rhetoric*. Mahwah, NJ: Paulist, 2000.

Wahlman, Maude. "Quilts, African American." In Appiah and Gates, *Africana*.

Wells, Junior. *Hoodoo Man Blues* (compact disc). Expanded ed. Delmark Records, 2011.

Wimbush, Vincent. "Interpreters: Enslaving/Enslaved/Runagate." *Journal of Biblical Literature* 130, no. 1 (2011): 5–24.

———. *White Men's Magic: Scripturalization as Slavery*. New York: Oxford University Press, 2012.

Yronwode, Catherine. *Hoodoo Herb and Root Magic: A Materia Magica of African-American Conjure*. Forestville, CA: Lucky Mojo Curio Co., 2002.

Zwerin, Mike. "Ornette Coleman and the Power of Harmolodics: Learning the Repertoire." *New York Times*, September 19, 2001. http://www.nytimes.com/2001/09/19/style/19iht-zwer19_ed2_.html.